AF390720

Title: Finance and Economics Made Simple
Subtitle: Your Essential Handbook to Parameters,
Formulas, and Their Consequences

Series: Understanding Money:
Finance and Economics Simplified
Author: Serenity Tanner

Table of Contents

Introduction
Purpose of the book

The purpose of this book is to provide a comprehensive guide to understanding the complex world of finance and economics. This book aims to break down the often intimidating and complicated formulas, parameters, and concepts into more manageable and understandable parts. Through the use of clear language and real-world examples, readers will gain a deeper understanding of the key components that make up the global financial and economic systems.

One of the primary purposes of this book is to provide readers with a solid foundation in the essential concepts and parameters of finance and economics. The book covers everything from macroeconomic parameters like Gross Domestic Product (GDP) and Inflation, to microeconomic parameters such as Market Structures and their Characteristics. Additionally, the book explores financial statements, investment analysis, and financial modeling, providing readers with a holistic understanding of the world of finance.

Another key purpose of this book is to empower readers with the knowledge to make informed decisions. Understanding the parameters and formulas of finance and economics is critical for anyone who wishes to invest, manage their finances, or work in a financial or economic capacity. This book is designed to equip readers with the knowledge and tools needed to confidently navigate the complex financial and economic landscape.

Ultimately, the purpose of this book is to provide readers with a comprehensive, accessible, and practical guide to understanding finance and economics. Whether you are a student, a professional, or simply interested in learning more about these essential topics, this book will provide you with the foundation and tools needed to succeed.

The target audience for this book is anyone who wants to understand the intricacies of finance and economics, from beginners to advanced learners. The book is designed to be accessible to individuals with little or no background in the subject matter, while still providing in-depth information for those with more advanced knowledge.

Students studying finance or economics at the undergraduate or graduate level will find this book to be an invaluable resource. It provides a comprehensive overview of the core concepts and theories that underpin the subject, making it an ideal companion for students throughout their academic journey.

Professionals in the finance and economics industries will also benefit from the knowledge provided in this book. It provides a detailed analysis of the key parameters and formulas used in the industry, making it a practical resource for those who are looking to apply their knowledge to real-world scenarios.

Entrepreneurs and business owners who are looking to start or grow their businesses will find the book to be an invaluable resource. It provides a detailed analysis of the key financial and economic concepts that underpin successful businesses, and provides practical advice on how to apply this knowledge to real-world scenarios.

Investors and analysts who are looking to make informed investment decisions will also find the book to be a useful resource. It provides a detailed analysis of key financial ratios and valuation metrics, as well as an overview of financial modeling and forecasting techniques, making it a practical resource for anyone who is looking to invest in the stock market or other financial instruments.

Overall, this book is intended for anyone who wants to gain a deep understanding of finance and economics, and how they impact the world around us. It provides a comprehensive overview of the key concepts and theories in the field, and is an essential resource for anyone who wants to succeed in the finance or economics industry.

This book is designed to provide a comprehensive guide to understanding the parameters, formulas, and their effects in finance and economics. The book is organized into six chapters, each covering a different aspect of finance and economics.

Chapter 1: Macroeconomic Parameters The first chapter of the book focuses on macroeconomic parameters such as Gross Domestic Product (GDP), inflation, unemployment rate, and balance of payments. The chapter provides an in-depth analysis of each parameter, including their components, significance, and how they affect the economy.

Chapter 2: Financial Parameters The second chapter delves into financial parameters such as interest rates, time value of money, present value, and the Capital Asset Pricing Model (CAPM). The chapter explores the meaning and importance of each parameter and how they are used in finance.

Chapter 3: Microeconomic Parameters The third chapter covers microeconomic parameters such as marginal utility and marginal cost, production function and its types, market structures, and price elasticity of demand and supply. This chapter explains how these parameters are used to understand the behavior of individual consumers and firms in the market.

Chapter 4: Financial Statements The fourth chapter provides an overview of financial statements such as balance sheet, income statement, cash flow statement, and financial ratios. The chapter explains the importance of these statements in analyzing a company's financial health and making investment decisions.

Chapter 5: Investment Analysis The fifth chapter focuses on investment analysis, covering topics such as net present value (NPV), internal rate of return (IRR), payback period, and capital budgeting process. This chapter explains how to evaluate investment opportunities using these parameters and how to make informed investment decisions.

Chapter 6: Financial Modeling The final chapter covers financial modeling, including spreadsheet modeling, Monte Carlo simulation, sensitivity analysis, and forecasting. This chapter explains how to build financial models using these techniques to make better financial decisions.

This book is intended for students, professionals, and anyone interested in learning about finance and economics. Whether you are a beginner or an experienced professional, this book will provide you with a comprehensive understanding of the parameters and formulas used in finance and economics.

Chapter 1: Macroeconomic Parameters
Gross Domestic Product (GDP) and its components

Gross Domestic Product (GDP) is one of the most important macroeconomic indicators used to measure the economic output of a country. It is defined as the market value of all final goods and services produced within a country during a specific period of time, usually a year or a quarter. GDP can be calculated using three different methods: the production approach, the expenditure approach, and the income approach.

The production approach measures GDP by adding up the value of all goods and services produced by different sectors of the economy. It involves calculating the value added at each stage of the production process, which is the difference between the value of the output produced and the value of the inputs used. For example, if a company produces a product worth $100 using raw materials that cost $50, the value added would be $50.

The expenditure approach measures GDP by adding up the value of all goods and services purchased by different sectors of the economy. It involves calculating the total spending on consumption, investment, government purchases, and net exports. Consumption refers to the spending by households on goods and services, investment refers to the spending by businesses on capital goods such as machinery and equipment, government purchases refer to the spending by the government on goods and services, and net exports refer to the difference between exports and imports.

The income approach measures GDP by adding up the income earned by different factors of production, such as labor and capital. It involves calculating the sum of wages, profits, rent, and interest earned in the production process.

GDP is made up of four main components: consumption, investment, government spending, and net exports. Consumption refers to the spending by households on goods and services, such as food, housing, and healthcare. Investment refers to the spending by businesses on capital goods, such as machinery and equipment, and on research and development. Government spending includes all spending by federal, state, and local governments on goods and services, such as education, defense, and infrastructure. Net exports refer to the difference between exports and imports, and can be positive or negative depending on whether a country is a net exporter or importer.

Understanding GDP and its components is essential for analyzing the health and performance of an economy. A growing GDP can indicate a strong and healthy economy, while a declining GDP can indicate a recession or economic downturn. By analyzing the components of GDP, policymakers and investors can identify areas of strength and weakness within an economy and make informed decisions about fiscal and monetary policies.

Inflation and deflation

Inflation and deflation are two important concepts in macroeconomics that are closely related to the overall health of an economy. Inflation refers to the general increase in the price level of goods and services in an economy over time, while deflation refers to the opposite: a decrease in the price level of goods and services over time.

Inflation can occur for a variety of reasons, including an increase in the money supply, increased demand for goods and services, or a decrease in the supply of goods and services. When inflation occurs, the purchasing power of money decreases, which means that consumers can buy fewer goods and services with the same amount of money. Inflation is typically measured by an inflation index, such as the Consumer Price Index (CPI), which tracks the changes in the prices of a basket of goods and services over time.

Deflation, on the other hand, can occur when there is a decrease in the demand for goods and services, or an increase in the supply of goods and services. Deflation can be caused by a variety of factors, including a decrease in consumer spending, a decrease in the money supply, or an increase in the supply of goods and services. When deflation occurs, the purchasing power of money increases, which means that consumers can buy more goods and services with the same amount of money.

Inflation and deflation can both have significant effects on an economy. High levels of inflation can lead to a decrease in consumer spending and investment, as consumers and investors become more cautious about spending money. In extreme cases, high levels of inflation can lead to hyperinflation, where prices increase rapidly and out of control, leading to economic instability and social unrest.

On the other hand, deflation can also have negative effects on an economy, as it can lead to a decrease in consumer spending and investment, which can lead to a decrease in production and employment. Deflation can also lead to an increase in the real value of debt, which can make it more difficult for borrowers to repay their debts.

Therefore, it is important for policymakers to carefully monitor inflation and deflation and take appropriate measures to ensure the stability of the economy. These measures may include adjusting interest rates, controlling the money supply, or implementing fiscal policy measures such as government spending and taxation.

Unemployment rate and its types

Unemployment is one of the key macroeconomic indicators that reflect the health of an economy. The unemployment rate is defined as the percentage of the labor force that is unemployed but actively seeking employment. This section will provide a detailed discussion of the concept of unemployment, its types, causes, and effects on the economy.

Types of Unemployment There are several types of unemployment that economists typically distinguish between, including frictional, structural, cyclical, and seasonal unemployment. Frictional unemployment occurs when workers are transitioning between jobs or entering the labor force for the first time. Structural unemployment is caused by a mismatch between the skills or location of workers and the available job openings. Cyclical unemployment results from the business cycle, as economic downturns lead to a decrease in demand for goods and services, which in turn leads to a decrease in demand for labor. Finally, seasonal unemployment is a type of unemployment that occurs due to seasonal changes in demand for labor, such as in agriculture or tourism.

Causes of Unemployment Unemployment can be caused by a variety of factors, both within and outside the control of individuals and businesses. For example, technological advancements can lead to the replacement of human labor with machines, resulting in job loss. Changes in consumer preferences or market demand can also result in job losses in specific industries. On the other hand, government policies such as minimum wage laws or regulations can increase the cost of hiring workers, leading to a decrease in employment.

Effects of Unemployment Unemployment has significant social and economic effects on individuals and the economy as a whole. For individuals, unemployment can lead to financial hardship, loss of self-esteem, and reduced quality of life. It can also lead to a lack of job skills and difficulty in re-entering the labor force. At the macroeconomic level, unemployment can lead to a decrease in consumer spending, a decline in tax revenues, and a decrease in economic growth.

In conclusion, understanding the concept of unemployment and its types, causes, and effects is crucial in assessing the health of an economy. Policymakers use this information to formulate economic policies that aim to reduce unemployment rates and improve the overall economic well-being of a society.

Balance of payments and its components

The balance of payments is a crucial macroeconomic parameter that measures a country's transactions with the rest of the world. It is a record of all the economic transactions between a country and its trading partners over a given period, usually a year.

The balance of payments is divided into three categories: current account, capital account, and financial account.

The current account measures a country's trade balance, including exports and imports of goods and services, net investment income, and net transfers. It reflects a country's economic health and competitiveness in international markets.

The capital account measures cross-border transactions related to non-produced, non-financial assets such as patents, copyrights, and trademarks.

The financial account measures cross-border transactions related to financial assets such as stocks, bonds, and loans. It includes foreign direct investment, portfolio investment, and other investments.

A positive balance of payments means that a country's receipts from exports and other inflows exceed its payments for imports and other outflows, indicating a surplus in the country's foreign exchange reserves. Conversely, a negative balance of payments means that a country's payments exceed its receipts, indicating a deficit in its foreign exchange reserves.

There are several factors that can impact a country's balance of payments, such as changes in exchange rates, trade policies, capital flows, and economic growth rates.

Understanding the components of the balance of payments is crucial for policymakers, investors, and analysts in assessing a country's economic performance and identifying potential risks and opportunities for growth.

The role of blockchain in macroeconomic analysis

Blockchain technology has gained a lot of attention in recent years due to its potential to revolutionize many aspects of modern society. In the field of macroeconomics, blockchain has the potential to transform the way we analyze and understand the economy.

One of the key benefits of blockchain technology is its ability to create a secure, decentralized ledger that can record transactions in a transparent and tamper-proof way. This has the potential to greatly improve the accuracy and transparency of economic data, which is essential for making informed policy decisions.

For example, blockchain-based systems could be used to track international trade flows and create a more accurate picture of the global economy. This could help policymakers to identify emerging trends and potential risks more quickly, and make more effective decisions as a result.

In addition, blockchain technology could also help to improve the efficiency and security of financial transactions. By creating a decentralized ledger that is resistant to hacking and fraud, blockchain-based systems could help to reduce the risk of financial crises and other systemic risks.

Despite these potential benefits, there are also some challenges associated with integrating blockchain into macroeconomic analysis. For example, the technology is still in its early stages and there are many technical and regulatory hurdles that need to be overcome before it can be widely adopted.

Furthermore, there are concerns about the potential impact of blockchain on traditional financial systems and the role of central banks in regulating the economy. As such, it is important to approach the integration of blockchain technology into macroeconomic analysis with caution and careful consideration.

Overall, while the role of blockchain in macroeconomic analysis is still uncertain, there is no doubt that it has the potential to transform the way we understand and analyze the economy. As such, it is important for economists and policymakers to stay up-to-date with the latest developments in blockchain technology and explore its potential applications in the field of macroeconomics.

Chapter 2: Financial Parameters
Interest rates and their types

Interest rates play a significant role in the financial market, affecting both borrowers and lenders. An interest rate is the amount charged by a lender to a borrower for the use of borrowed money, usually expressed as a percentage of the principal amount. In this section, we will discuss interest rates and their types.

Firstly, it is important to understand the concept of nominal interest rates and real interest rates. Nominal interest rates are the rates quoted by lenders and are not adjusted for inflation. In contrast, real interest rates are adjusted for inflation, and reflect the true cost of borrowing or the real return on lending.

There are several types of interest rates, including simple interest rates, compound interest rates, and effective interest rates. Simple interest rates are calculated as a percentage of the principal amount, and do not take into account any interest that accrues on the interest earned. Compound interest rates, on the other hand, take into account the interest earned on the principal amount as well as the interest earned on any interest that accrues over time. Effective interest rates are the true rates of return earned or paid, and take into account the compounding of interest over time.

In addition, interest rates can be classified as fixed or variable. Fixed interest rates remain the same throughout the life of the loan or investment, while variable interest rates can change based on market conditions or other factors.

Interest rates have a significant impact on the financial market, including stock prices, bond prices, and exchange rates. In general, when interest rates rise, the prices of bonds and stocks may decline, while the value of currencies may increase.

Overall, understanding interest rates and their types is essential for investors, lenders, and borrowers alike. By understanding how interest rates work, individuals can make informed decisions regarding their investments and borrowing strategies.

Time value of money

Time value of money is a fundamental concept in finance, which states that the value of money changes over time. This concept is based on the idea that a dollar received today is worth more than a dollar received in the future, due to the potential to invest that money and earn a return.

The time value of money is important in financial decision-making, as it helps individuals and organizations determine the value of future cash flows and investments. It is used to calculate the present value of future cash flows, and to determine the amount of money that needs to be invested today to achieve a desired future value.

One of the key tools used to calculate the time value of money is the concept of discounting. Discounting is the process of adjusting future cash flows to their present value, based on an assumed discount rate. The discount rate represents the cost of capital, or the expected return that an investor could earn on an alternative investment with similar risk.

The time value of money is also used to calculate the future value of investments, such as bonds or annuities. The future value is the value of an investment at a future point in time, assuming a specified rate of return. This calculation is important for individuals and organizations that are planning for retirement or other long-term goals.

In addition to its use in financial decision-making, the time value of money has broader implications for the economy as a whole. It helps to explain the impact of inflation on the value of money over time, and the role of interest rates in shaping economic growth and investment.

Overall, a solid understanding of the time value of money is essential for anyone working in finance or economics. It is a key building block for financial analysis, investment management, and economic forecasting.

Present value and future value

Present value (PV) and future value (FV) are fundamental concepts in finance that allow us to understand the time value of money. Present value refers to the current worth of a future cash flow or sum of money, whereas future value refers to the expected value of an investment at a future date, assuming a specific interest rate.

The concept of present value can be used in various financial calculations, such as determining the value of a bond, evaluating investment opportunities, and calculating the value of an annuity. It is based on the principle that money available today is worth more than the same amount of money available in the future, due to the potential to earn interest or returns on the investment.

The formula for present value is:

$$PV = FV / (1 + r)^n$$

where PV is the present value, FV is the future value, r is the discount rate, and n is the number of periods.

Similarly, the concept of future value can be used to calculate the value of an investment over time. The formula for future value is:

$$FV = PV \times (1 + r)^n$$

where FV is the future value, PV is the present value, r is the interest rate, and n is the number of periods.

Understanding present value and future value is crucial in making investment decisions, as it helps us determine the potential return on an investment and compare different investment opportunities. These concepts are also important in financial planning, such as retirement planning, where individuals need to calculate the value of their savings at different points in the future.

In addition, present value and future value can be used in combination with other financial parameters, such as interest rates and inflation, to evaluate the potential risk and return of an investment.

Overall, understanding present value and future value is essential in finance and economics, as these concepts form the foundation for various financial calculations and investment decisions.

Capital asset pricing model (CAPM)

Capital Asset Pricing Model (CAPM) is a widely used financial model that helps investors and analysts to calculate the expected return on an investment by taking into account the risk-free rate of return, the expected market return, and the asset's beta, which measures its volatility relative to the market.

The CAPM was first introduced by William Sharpe in 1964 and has since become a cornerstone of modern portfolio theory. The model assumes that investors are rational and risk-averse, meaning that they seek to maximize returns while minimizing risk. The model also assumes that investors have access to all relevant information and can trade freely without transaction costs.

The CAPM is based on the concept of the Security Market Line (SML), which is a graphical representation of the relationship between the expected return and the beta of an asset. The SML shows that the expected return on an asset increases as its beta increases, indicating that higher-risk assets should have higher expected returns.

To calculate the expected return on an asset using the CAPM, the following formula is used:

Expected Return = Risk-Free Rate + Beta x (Expected Market Return - Risk-Free Rate)

Where:

- Risk-Free Rate: The rate of return on a risk-free investment such as government bonds

- Beta: A measure of the volatility of an asset relative to the overall market

- Expected Market Return: The expected rate of return on the market as a whole

The CAPM has several limitations and criticisms. One of the main criticisms is that it relies on several key assumptions that may not hold true in the real world, such as the assumption of rational and risk-averse investors. Additionally, the model does not account for the impact of other factors that may affect an asset's return, such as market sentiment and changes in economic conditions.

Despite its limitations, the CAPM remains a popular tool for estimating the expected return on an investment and is widely used in finance and investment analysis. It provides a simple and intuitive way to evaluate the risk and return of an investment and helps investors to make informed decisions about their portfolio allocation.

How digital assets and cryptocurrency impact financial parameters

As digital assets and cryptocurrencies gain increasing acceptance, it becomes imperative to consider their impact on financial parameters. A number of financial parameters such as interest rates, exchange rates, and inflation are affected by the usage and popularity of digital assets and cryptocurrencies.

One key aspect of digital assets and cryptocurrencies is their decentralization, which means they are not controlled by a central authority. This creates a unique challenge for regulators, who are tasked with creating rules and guidelines to ensure the stability of financial markets.

Interest rates are one of the key financial parameters impacted by digital assets and cryptocurrencies. In traditional finance, central banks control interest rates by setting the benchmark interest rate for their respective economies. However, with the rise of digital assets and cryptocurrencies, the decentralized nature of these assets means that traditional methods of controlling interest rates are no longer effective. As a result, central banks are now forced to consider the impact of digital assets and cryptocurrencies on interest rates.

Exchange rates are another key financial parameter impacted by digital assets and cryptocurrencies. Digital assets and cryptocurrencies are traded on decentralized exchanges, which are not subject to the same regulations as traditional exchanges. As a result, the value of digital assets and cryptocurrencies can fluctuate wildly, leading to increased volatility in exchange rates.

Inflation is also impacted by digital assets and cryptocurrencies. Digital assets and cryptocurrencies are often touted as a hedge against inflation due to their limited supply. For example, Bitcoin has a fixed supply of 21 million coins, which means that it is not subject to inflation in the same way that fiat currencies are. This has led to increased interest in digital assets and cryptocurrencies as a potential hedge against inflation.

However, digital assets and cryptocurrencies can also contribute to inflation in certain circumstances. For example, when digital assets and cryptocurrencies are used for speculative purposes, it can lead to a bubble that eventually bursts, resulting in inflation.

Overall, the impact of digital assets and cryptocurrencies on financial parameters is complex and multifaceted. While they offer potential benefits such as increased efficiency and a hedge against inflation, they also pose significant challenges for regulators and traditional financial institutions. As digital assets and cryptocurrencies continue to gain acceptance, it will be important for regulators and financial institutions to stay abreast of the latest developments in order to effectively manage the impact of these assets on financial parameters.

Chapter 3: Microeconomic Parameters
Marginal utility and marginal cost

Marginal utility and marginal cost are two essential microeconomic concepts that are used to explain the behavior of consumers and producers in a market. Marginal utility is the additional satisfaction or benefit that a consumer derives from consuming an extra unit of a good or service. On the other hand, marginal cost is the additional cost incurred by a firm or producer when they produce an extra unit of a good or service. In this section, we will explore these concepts in greater detail.

Marginal Utility:

Marginal utility can be understood as the increase in total utility a consumer gets when they consume an additional unit of a good or service. Total utility is the satisfaction or happiness that a consumer gets from consuming a certain amount of a good or service. The law of diminishing marginal utility states that as a consumer consumes more units of a good or service, the marginal utility derived from each additional unit decreases. This means that as the consumer has more of a good, the value they place on each additional unit decreases.

For instance, let's say that a consumer is hungry and they decide to eat a pizza. The first slice of pizza they eat will give them a lot of satisfaction, and they might feel quite happy after eating it. However, as they eat more slices, their satisfaction level will gradually decrease, and they will not feel as happy after each slice they eat. Eventually, they will reach a point where they will be full, and even if they eat another slice, they will not feel any additional satisfaction.

Marginal Cost:

Marginal cost is the additional cost incurred by a producer when they produce an extra unit of a good or service. The marginal cost of production is important because it helps firms determine the optimal level of production. The law of increasing marginal cost states that as a firm produces more units of a good or service, the marginal cost of producing each additional unit increases. This means that it becomes more expensive for the firm to produce each additional unit.

For instance, let's say that a firm produces t-shirts. The cost of producing the first t-shirt might be high because the firm has to pay for materials, labor, and other costs associated with production. However, as they produce more t-shirts, they might be able to take advantage of economies of scale, which means that the cost of production decreases as the volume of production increases. But at some point, the cost of production will start to increase again due to factors such as diminishing returns or limited resources.

Conclusion:

Marginal utility and marginal cost are two essential concepts in microeconomics that help us understand how consumers and producers make decisions in a market. The law of diminishing marginal utility and the law of increasing marginal cost both explain why consumers and firms are willing to pay a certain price for a good or service. In general, consumers are willing to pay more for goods or services that provide them with high marginal utility, while firms are willing to produce more of a good or service as long as the marginal cost of production is less than the market price. Understanding these concepts is crucial for analyzing market behavior and making informed economic decisions.

Production function and its types

Production function is an essential concept in microeconomics, which describes the relationship between inputs and outputs in a production process. The production function specifies how much output can be produced from a given set of inputs, such as labor and capital, and how these inputs should be combined to achieve maximum efficiency. In this section, we will discuss the production function and its different types.

The production function is typically represented by the following equation:

$$Q = f(L, K)$$

Where Q represents the quantity of output produced, L represents the quantity of labor used, and K represents the quantity of capital used. The production function can also include other inputs, such as raw materials, energy, and technology.

There are different types of production functions that reflect different ways in which inputs are combined to produce output. These include:

1. Linear Production Function: The linear production function assumes that the relationship between inputs and output is linear. This means that each additional unit of input contributes equally to the output. For example, if two units of labor and two units of capital produce 10 units of output, then four units of labor and four units of capital would produce 20 units of output.

2. Cobb-Douglas Production Function: The Cobb-Douglas production function assumes that the relationship between inputs and output is non-linear. This means that each additional unit of input contributes less to the output than the previous unit. The function is represented as:

$$Q = AK^aL^b$$

Where Q is the quantity of output, K is the quantity of capital, L is the quantity of labor, A is a constant, and a and b are coefficients that determine the relative importance of capital and labor in the production process.

3. Leontief Production Function: The Leontief production function assumes that the relationship between inputs and output is fixed. This means that output can only be increased by adding more of all inputs in the same proportion. The function is represented as:

$$Q = \min (aL, bK)$$

Where Q is the quantity of output, L is the quantity of labor, K is the quantity of capital, and a and b are coefficients that determine the minimum quantity of each input required to produce a unit of output.

4. CES Production Function: The CES (Constant Elasticity of Substitution) production function assumes that inputs can be substituted for each other to a certain extent. The function is represented as:

$$Q = (aL^{-r} + bK^{-r})^{-1/r}$$

Where Q is the quantity of output, L is the quantity of labor, K is the quantity of capital, a and b are coefficients that determine the elasticity of substitution between labor and capital, and r is the degree of substitutability between the inputs.

In conclusion, the production function is a critical concept in microeconomics that helps to determine the most efficient way of producing output using available inputs. There are different types of production functions, each with its unique characteristics that reflect the way inputs are combined to produce output. Understanding these functions is crucial for firms to make optimal production decisions and for policymakers to design effective industrial policies.

Market structures and their characteristics

Market structures are a fundamental concept in microeconomics that describe the characteristics of different types of markets. In this chapter, we will discuss the four main types of market structures: perfect competition, monopolistic competition, oligopoly, and monopoly.

Perfect competition is a market structure in which there are many small firms that sell identical products. There are no barriers to entry or exit in a perfectly competitive market, and all firms are price-takers. In other words, they have no control over the market price and must accept the prevailing market price. Perfect competition is characterized by low profit margins, efficient production, and no market power for any individual firm.

Monopolistic competition is a market structure in which there are many small firms that sell differentiated products. Each firm has a small degree of market power due to the uniqueness of its product, but there are still low barriers to entry and exit. Firms in monopolistic competition compete based on product differentiation, marketing, and branding. Monopolistic competition is characterized by higher profit margins than perfect competition, but also less efficiency in production.

Oligopoly is a market structure in which a few large firms dominate the market. These firms have significant market power, which means they can influence the market price. Oligopolies often engage in strategic behavior such as collusion or price-fixing, which can lead to higher profits for the firms but may harm consumers. There are often significant barriers to entry in an oligopoly, such as high startup costs or government regulations.

Monopoly is a market structure in which there is only one firm that dominates the market. This firm has complete market power and can set the market price. Monopolies often arise due to barriers to entry such as patents, control over key resources, or economies of scale. Monopolies can be harmful to consumers due to the lack of competition, which can lead to higher prices and lower quality products.

Understanding market structures is essential for firms, policymakers, and consumers. Firms need to understand their position in the market and how to compete effectively, policymakers need to regulate markets to ensure fair competition and protect consumers, and consumers need to make informed decisions based on the market structure and characteristics of the products they purchase.

In conclusion, this chapter provides an overview of the four main types of market structures and their characteristics. By understanding the different types of market structures, we can better understand how markets operate and how firms, policymakers, and consumers can make better decisions.

Price elasticity of demand and supply

Price elasticity of demand and supply is a crucial concept in microeconomics that helps to understand the responsiveness of buyers and sellers to changes in market prices. Elasticity measures the percentage change in quantity demanded or supplied in response to a percentage change in price. This concept is essential in determining the optimal pricing strategy for businesses, predicting the impact of tax policies on markets, and analyzing the behavior of consumers and producers in different market structures.

Price Elasticity of Demand:

Price elasticity of demand (PED) measures the responsiveness of quantity demanded to changes in price. PED is calculated as the percentage change in quantity demanded divided by the percentage change in price. If PED is greater than one, demand is said to be elastic, which means that a small change in price will result in a relatively larger change in quantity demanded. If PED is less than one, demand is said to be inelastic, which means that a change in price will result in a relatively smaller change in quantity demanded. When PED is equal to one, demand is said to be unit elastic.

The factors that affect the elasticity of demand include the availability of substitutes, the proportion of income spent on the good, and the time period under consideration. Goods with close substitutes tend to have more elastic demand because consumers can easily switch to the substitutes if the price of the good increases. In contrast, goods that make up a small proportion of consumers' income tend to have inelastic demand because consumers are less sensitive to changes in the price of these goods. Finally, the longer the time period under consideration, the more elastic the demand because consumers have more time to adjust their behavior and find substitutes.

Price Elasticity of Supply:

Price elasticity of supply (PES) measures the responsiveness of quantity supplied to changes in price. PES is calculated as the percentage change in quantity supplied divided by the percentage change in price. If PES is greater than one, supply is said to be elastic, which means that a small change in price will result in a relatively larger change in quantity supplied. If PES is less than one, supply is said to be inelastic, which means that a change in price will result in a relatively smaller change in quantity supplied. When PES is equal to one, supply is said to be unit elastic.

The factors that affect the elasticity of supply include the availability of inputs, the time period under consideration, and the ease of entry and exit into the market. Goods that require specialized inputs or have limited availability of inputs tend to have inelastic supply because producers are less able to adjust their production in response to changes in price. Similarly, goods that have a short production cycle or are produced using readily available inputs tend to have elastic supply. Finally, markets with low barriers to entry and exit tend to have more elastic supply because new producers can easily enter the market in response to higher prices, increasing the supply.

Applications of Price Elasticity:

Price elasticity has numerous applications in microeconomics, including in pricing strategies for businesses, tax policy, and consumer and producer behavior in different market structures. Businesses can use price elasticity to determine the optimal pricing strategy for their products. For example, if the demand for a product is elastic, a small reduction in price can result in a larger increase in sales, leading to higher overall revenue. On the other hand, if the demand is inelastic, a small increase in price may not result in a significant reduction in quantity demanded, allowing the business to charge a higher price and increase profits.

Price elasticity is also relevant for tax policy. Goods with inelastic demand, such as gasoline and cigarettes, are often taxed at a higher rate because consumers are less likely to reduce their consumption in response to the tax. Conversely, goods with elastic demand, such as fruits and vegetables, are less likely to be heavily taxed because consumers are more likely to reduce their consumption in response to the tax. Tax policy makers need to understand the price elasticity of demand in order to determine the appropriate tax rate and the revenue that can be generated from it. Similarly, price elasticity of supply plays a significant role in determining the behavior of producers. If a product has an elastic supply, producers can quickly increase their production in response to a price increase, resulting in a relatively small increase in price. However, if a product has an inelastic supply, such as limited resources like land or minerals, a price increase can result in a significant increase in the product's price. Understanding the price elasticity of supply helps businesses make informed decisions about production levels and pricing strategies.

The role of blockchain in microeconomic analysis

Blockchain technology has the potential to revolutionize microeconomic analysis in various ways. One of the most significant applications of blockchain technology in microeconomics is through the development of smart contracts. Smart contracts are self-executing contracts with the terms of the agreement between buyer and seller being directly written into lines of code. They allow for the automation of certain processes that would traditionally require intermediaries, such as banks or lawyers, to execute. The use of smart contracts reduces transaction costs and enhances efficiency.

In microeconomic analysis, the use of smart contracts can facilitate the analysis of market data, as transactions and other economic activities are recorded on the blockchain in real-time. These transactions can be analyzed to provide insights into consumer behavior, including purchasing patterns and the elasticity of demand. Moreover, blockchain technology can enable microeconomic researchers to gather data from a wider range of sources, including data that was previously inaccessible.

Another application of blockchain technology in microeconomics is the development of decentralized marketplaces. These marketplaces allow for direct transactions between buyers and sellers, without the need for intermediaries. The use of decentralized marketplaces has the potential to reduce transaction costs and increase efficiency, particularly in markets that are traditionally opaque, such as the art market.

Blockchain technology can also facilitate the development of more efficient supply chains. The use of blockchain technology in supply chains allows for the tracking of goods from their origin to their final destination. This level of transparency can help reduce transaction costs and increase efficiency, particularly in industries with complex supply chains, such as the food and pharmaceutical industries.

Finally, blockchain technology can be used to facilitate peer-to-peer lending, thereby reducing the need for intermediaries such as banks. Peer-to-peer lending platforms allow borrowers to obtain loans from individual lenders, without the need for traditional financial institutions. This type of lending can help reduce transaction costs and increase access to credit, particularly for individuals who may have difficulty obtaining loans through traditional financial institutions.

In conclusion, blockchain technology has the potential to revolutionize microeconomic analysis by reducing transaction costs, increasing efficiency, and providing researchers with access to new sources of data. The development of smart contracts, decentralized marketplaces, efficient supply chains, and peer-to-peer lending platforms are just a few examples of how blockchain technology is changing the way we think about microeconomics. As blockchain technology continues to evolve, it is likely that we will see even more applications of this technology in the field of microeconomics.

The balance sheet is a financial statement that provides a snapshot of a company's financial position at a specific point in time. It is a summary of the company's assets, liabilities, and equity. The balance sheet is also known as the statement of financial position.

The balance sheet is divided into two sections: assets and liabilities + equity. The assets section lists all the resources that the company owns or has a claim to. These resources can be classified as current or non-current assets. Current assets are expected to be used up or converted into cash within a year, while non-current assets are expected to be used up over a longer period.

The most common types of current assets are cash, accounts receivable, inventory, and prepaid expenses. Cash is the most liquid asset and includes money in bank accounts and cash on hand. Accounts receivable are amounts owed to the company by customers for goods or services provided. Inventory includes raw materials, work in progress, and finished goods. Prepaid expenses are payments made for services that will be received in the future, such as insurance or rent.

Non-current assets include property, plant, and equipment (PPE), investments, and intangible assets. PPE includes land, buildings, machinery, and equipment. Investments include stocks and bonds that the company holds for a long-term purpose. Intangible assets include patents, copyrights, trademarks, and goodwill.

The liabilities + equity section of the balance sheet lists the company's debts and obligations. Like assets, liabilities can also be classified as current or non-current. Current liabilities are those that are expected to be paid off or settled within a year, while non-current liabilities are expected to be paid off over a longer period.

The most common types of current liabilities are accounts payable, short-term loans, and accrued expenses. Accounts payable are amounts owed by the company to suppliers for goods or services received. Short-term loans are loans that are expected to be repaid within a year. Accrued expenses are expenses that have been incurred but not yet paid, such as salaries and wages.

Non-current liabilities include long-term debt, deferred tax liabilities, and pension liabilities. Long-term debt includes loans and bonds that are expected to be repaid over a longer period. Deferred tax liabilities arise when a company's taxable income is less than its accounting income, resulting in lower taxes paid in the short-term but higher taxes in the long-term. Pension liabilities arise when a company has promised to pay its employees a pension after they retire.

The equity section of the balance sheet shows the owners' stake in the company. It includes the amount of capital contributed by the owners and any retained earnings. Retained earnings are profits that have not been paid out as dividends.

In summary, the balance sheet provides a comprehensive view of a company's financial position by listing all its assets, liabilities, and equity at a specific point in time. It is an important tool for investors, creditors, and other stakeholders to assess the company's financial health and performance.

Income statement and its components

Introduction: An income statement, also known as a profit and loss statement, is a financial statement that reports a company's revenues, expenses, gains, and losses over a specific period. It is one of the most important financial statements as it provides insights into a company's profitability and overall financial performance. In this section, we will discuss the different components of an income statement and how they are used to evaluate a company's financial health.

Revenue: Revenue, also known as sales or turnover, is the total amount of money a company earns from selling its products or services. It is the first item listed on an income statement and is reported for a specific period, such as a quarter or a year. Revenue is a critical metric for evaluating a company's financial performance, as it indicates the level of demand for its products or services.

Cost of Goods Sold (COGS): Cost of goods sold, also known as cost of sales, is the cost associated with producing and delivering a company's products or services. It includes the cost of materials, labor, and overhead expenses related to the production process. COGS is subtracted from revenue to determine a company's gross profit.

Gross Profit: Gross profit is the difference between revenue and cost of goods sold. It is an important metric for evaluating a company's profitability at the product level. A high gross profit margin indicates that a company is effectively controlling its production costs, while a low gross profit margin may indicate inefficiencies in the production process.

Operating Expenses: Operating expenses are the costs associated with running a company's day-to-day operations. They include expenses such as salaries, rent, utilities, and marketing expenses. Operating expenses are subtracted from gross profit to determine a company's operating profit.

Operating Profit: Operating profit, also known as earnings before interest and taxes (EBIT), is the profit a company generates from its core operations. It is calculated by subtracting operating expenses from gross profit. Operating profit is a critical metric for evaluating a company's operating efficiency and profitability.

Interest Expense: Interest expense is the cost associated with borrowing money. It is reported on the income statement as a separate line item and is subtracted from operating profit to determine a company's earnings before taxes.

Earnings Before Taxes (EBT): Earnings before taxes, also known as pre-tax income, is the profit a company generates before paying income taxes. It is calculated by subtracting interest expense from operating profit.

Income Tax Expense: Income tax expense is the amount a company owes in taxes to the government. It is reported on the income statement as a separate line item and is subtracted from earnings before taxes to determine a company's net income.

Net Income: Net income, also known as net profit, is the profit a company generates after paying all its expenses, including taxes. It is calculated by subtracting income tax expense from earnings before taxes. Net income is a critical metric for evaluating a company's overall financial health and profitability.

Conclusion: An income statement is a critical financial statement that provides insights into a company's financial performance. By analyzing the different components of an income statement, investors and analysts can evaluate a company's revenue, profitability, and overall financial health. Understanding the various components of an income statement is essential for making informed investment decisions and assessing a company's financial health.

Cash flow statement and its components

Introduction: The cash flow statement is a financial statement that provides information about the inflow and outflow of cash within an organization during a specific period. It reflects the actual movement of cash and cash equivalents and helps in determining the liquidity of a company. This chapter will cover the components of the cash flow statement and their significance in financial analysis.

Components of the Cash Flow Statement: The cash flow statement comprises three components, namely operating activities, investing activities, and financing activities. These components help in identifying the sources and uses of cash for an organization.

Operating Activities: The operating activities section of the cash flow statement provides information about the cash inflows and outflows resulting from the primary business activities of the organization. It includes the cash received from the sale of goods and services, payment to suppliers and employees, and other expenses related to the operating activities. Operating activities generate the primary source of cash flow for most businesses.

Investing Activities: Investing activities refer to the cash inflows and outflows related to the purchase and sale of long-term assets such as property, plant, and equipment, as well as investments in other companies. These activities are essential for the growth of a company but do not generate cash in the short term. Investing activities can have a significant impact on the cash flow statement.

Financing Activities: Financing activities refer to the cash inflows and outflows related to the raising and repaying of funds. These activities include the issuance of shares, repayment of loans, payment of dividends, and other activities related to the financing of the organization. Financing activities have a significant impact on the capital structure of a company.

Significance of Cash Flow Statement in Financial Analysis: The cash flow statement is an essential tool for financial analysis as it provides information about the liquidity and solvency of an organization. It helps in determining the sources and uses of cash, which can be used to evaluate the ability of a company to meet its obligations. The following are some of the key ratios derived from the cash flow statement that can be used in financial analysis:

- Operating cash flow ratio: This ratio is used to determine the ability of a company to generate cash from its operations. It is calculated as operating cash flow divided by current liabilities.

- Cash debt coverage ratio: This ratio is used to determine the ability of a company to repay its debt using its cash flow. It is calculated as operating cash flow divided by total debt.

- Free cash flow: This represents the amount of cash generated after deducting capital expenditures. It is used to evaluate the ability of a company to generate cash for future growth opportunities.

Conclusion: The cash flow statement is a crucial financial statement that provides information about the inflow and outflow of cash within an organization during a specific period. It helps in determining the liquidity and solvency of a company and provides valuable information for financial analysis. The operating activities, investing activities, and financing activities are the key components of the cash flow statement, and each of them plays a vital role in determining the financial health of an organization.

Introduction Financial ratios are important tools for analyzing and evaluating a company's financial performance. Financial ratios provide a quick snapshot of a company's financial health and can be used to compare the performance of one company to another or to an industry average. This chapter will discuss the most commonly used financial ratios, their significance, and how they are calculated.

Types of Financial Ratios There are several types of financial ratios that can be calculated. These ratios can be grouped into categories based on what they measure. The categories include profitability ratios, liquidity ratios, solvency ratios, and efficiency ratios.

Profitability Ratios Profitability ratios measure a company's ability to generate profits. These ratios are important to investors as they provide an indication of the company's financial health and its ability to generate a return on investment. The most commonly used profitability ratios are:

1. Gross Profit Margin: This ratio measures the percentage of revenue that remains after deducting the cost of goods sold. A high gross profit margin indicates that the company is able to sell its products at a higher price than its cost of production.

2. Net Profit Margin: This ratio measures the percentage of revenue that rcmains after all expenses, including taxes, interest, and depreciation, are deducted. A high net profit margin indicates that the company is able to control its expenses and generate a higher profit.

3. Return on Equity (ROE): This ratio measures the percentage return that shareholders receive on their investment in the company. A high ROE indicates that the company is generating a higher return on investment for its shareholders.

Liquidity Ratios Liquidity ratios measure a company's ability to meet its short-term financial obligations. These ratios are important to creditors as they provide an indication of the company's ability to repay its debts. The most commonly used liquidity ratios are:

1. Current Ratio: This ratio measures a company's ability to pay its current liabilities with its current assets. A high current ratio indicates that the company has sufficient assets to pay its debts in the short-term.

2. Quick Ratio: This ratio measures a company's ability to pay its current liabilities with its most liquid assets, such as cash and marketable securities. A high quick ratio indicates that the company has sufficient liquid assets to pay its debts in the short-term.

Solvency Ratios Solvency ratios measure a company's ability to meet its long-term financial obligations. These ratios are important to investors as they provide an indication of the company's financial health in the long-term. The most commonly used solvency ratios are:

1. Debt-to-Equity Ratio: This ratio measures the proportion of debt to equity in a company's capital structure. A high debt-to-equity ratio indicates that the company is relying heavily on debt to finance its operations.

2. Interest Coverage Ratio: This ratio measures a company's ability to pay its interest expenses. A high interest coverage ratio indicates that the company has sufficient earnings to cover its interest expenses.

Efficiency Ratios Efficiency ratios measure a company's ability to manage its assets and liabilities to generate revenue. These ratios are important to investors as they provide an indication of the company's ability to generate revenue from its assets. The most commonly used efficiency ratios are:

1. Asset Turnover Ratio: This ratio measures the amount of revenue generated for every dollar of assets a company has. A high asset turnover ratio indicates that the company is using its assets efficiently to generate revenue.

2. Inventory Turnover Ratio: This ratio measures the number of times a company sells and replaces its inventory within a given period. A high inventory turnover ratio indicates that the company is efficiently managing its inventory.

Conclusion Financial ratios are important tools for analyzing and evaluating a company's financial performance. The most commonly used financial ratios include profitability ratios, liquidity ratios, solvency ratios,

How blockchain technology is disrupting financial statements

Blockchain technology has the potential to disrupt many industries, including finance and accounting. Blockchain's ability to create a tamper-proof, decentralized ledger makes it an ideal tool for tracking financial transactions and creating transparent financial statements. In this section, we will explore how blockchain technology is disrupting financial statements and what benefits it brings to the table.

Decentralized ledgers

One of the most significant benefits of using blockchain technology in financial statements is the creation of decentralized ledgers. In traditional accounting, a single entity is responsible for maintaining and verifying the accuracy of financial records. This centralized approach can be vulnerable to fraud, errors, or even data breaches. By contrast, blockchain technology creates a decentralized ledger, which means that the records are distributed across a network of nodes, making it much harder for an attacker to tamper with the data.

Immutable records

Another key benefit of using blockchain technology in financial statements is the ability to create immutable records. Blockchain technology creates an audit trail of transactions that are recorded on the blockchain. Once a transaction has been recorded, it cannot be deleted or modified. This ensures that the data in the financial statements is accurate and tamper-proof.

Smart contracts

Smart contracts are self-executing contracts that are programmed on the blockchain. They can be used to automate financial transactions, including those involved in creating financial statements. For example, a smart contract can be programmed to automatically execute a payment when certain conditions are met, such as a specified date or a predefined threshold. Smart contracts can also be used to create automated financial statements that can be audited in real-time.

Transparency

Blockchain technology provides unprecedented transparency in financial transactions. Every transaction is recorded on the blockchain, creating an unalterable record of every financial transaction. This creates a transparent financial ecosystem that is beneficial for businesses, investors, and regulators alike. It can help to reduce fraud, increase trust, and improve the accuracy of financial statements.

Cost savings

Blockchain technology can also help to reduce the cost of preparing financial statements. By automating the process of creating and verifying financial transactions, blockchain technology can reduce the need for manual labor, which can be a significant cost-saving measure for businesses. Additionally, because blockchain technology creates an immutable ledger, it can also reduce the cost of auditing financial statements.

Challenges

Despite the potential benefits of using blockchain technology in financial statements, there are some challenges that need to be addressed. One of the challenges is the lack of standardization in the blockchain ecosystem. Different blockchains have different capabilities and requirements, which can make it difficult to create a standardized approach to financial reporting.

Another challenge is the need for specialized skills and knowledge. Blockchain technology is relatively new, and there is a shortage of skilled professionals who can implement and manage blockchain systems. Additionally, there is a need for more education and training on the benefits and risks of using blockchain technology in financial statements.

Conclusion

Blockchain technology has the potential to disrupt the financial statements industry, providing new levels of transparency, security, and cost savings. It can help to reduce fraud, increase trust, and improve the accuracy of financial statements. However, there are challenges that need to be addressed, such as the lack of standardization and the need for specialized skills and knowledge. Overall, the use of blockchain technology in financial statements is an exciting development that has the potential to transform the accounting and finance industry.

Net present value (NPV) and its significance

Net Present Value (NPV) is an investment analysis technique used to determine the potential profitability of a project or investment by comparing the present value of its expected cash inflows to the present value of its expected cash outflows. In this section, we will explore the concept of NPV, its significance in investment analysis, and the key factors that impact its calculation.

Understanding Net Present Value (NPV)

The concept of NPV is based on the principle that the value of money changes over time due to inflation, interest rates, and other economic factors. Therefore, the future cash inflows and outflows of an investment or project need to be adjusted to reflect their present value.

The formula for calculating NPV is as follows:

$$NPV = CF_0 + CF_1 / (1+r) + CF_2 / (1+r)^2 + \ldots + CF_n / (1+r)^n$$

Where, CF_0 = cash flow in year zero (usually the initial investment) CF_1 to CF_n = cash flows in years 1 to n r = discount rate

The discount rate represents the opportunity cost of investing in the project, i.e., the rate of return that could be earned by investing in a similar project or security with similar risks. The higher the discount rate, the lower the present value of future cash flows, and vice versa.

If the NPV is positive, the investment is expected to generate returns greater than the required rate of return (i.e., the discount rate). A negative NPV indicates that the investment is expected to generate returns lower than the required rate of return, and may not be a viable investment.

Significance of Net Present Value (NPV)

NPV is a widely used investment analysis tool that helps investors and analysts to evaluate the potential profitability of a project or investment. Some of the key benefits of using NPV include:

Evaluating the feasibility of an investment

NPV helps investors to determine whether an investment is worth pursuing by comparing its expected returns to the required rate of return. If the NPV is positive, the investment is expected to generate returns greater than the required rate of return and may be considered feasible.

Comparing different investment opportunities

NPV can be used to compare different investment opportunities by calculating the NPV of each opportunity and selecting the one with the highest NPV. This helps investors to choose the most profitable investment opportunity.

Accounting for the time value of money

NPV adjusts the future cash inflows and outflows to reflect their present value, taking into account the time value of money. This helps investors to make informed investment decisions by considering the impact of inflation and other economic factors.

Incorporating risk into investment analysis

NPV can be adjusted to account for the level of risk associated with an investment by using a higher discount rate. This helps investors to evaluate the potential returns and risks of an investment and make informed decisions.

Factors Affecting Net Present Value (NPV)

Several factors can impact the calculation of NPV, including:

Discount rate

The discount rate is a key factor that impacts the calculation of NPV. A higher discount rate will result in a lower present value of future cash flows, reducing the NPV.

Conversely, a lower discount rate will result in a higher present value of future cash flows, increasing the NPV.

Cash flows

The cash flows generated by an investment or project are also a critical factor that impacts the calculation of NPV. Higher cash flows will result in a higher NPV, while lower cash flows will result in a lower NPV.

Time horizon

The time horizon of an investment or project is also an important factor that impacts the calculation of NPV. Longer-term investments will generally have a higher NPV due to the compounding effect of future cash flows. However, the longer the time horizon, the greater the uncertainty and risk associated with the investment. This uncertainty and risk can be incorporated into the calculation of NPV through the use of a discount rate that reflects the riskiness of the investment. A higher discount rate would be applied to riskier investments with longer time horizons, resulting in a lower NPV. On the other hand, a lower discount rate would be applied to less risky investments with shorter time horizons, resulting in a higher NPV.

It is important to note that NPV is not the only investment analysis tool available. Other popular tools include internal rate of return (IRR), payback period, and profitability index. However, NPV is often considered to be the most accurate and comprehensive tool for investment analysis, as it takes into account the time value of money, cash flows, and the cost of capital.

Investors and businesses use NPV analysis to evaluate potential investment opportunities and determine whether they are financially viable. A positive NPV indicates that the investment is expected to generate a return greater than the required rate of return, and therefore, it is considered financially attractive. A negative NPV, on the other hand, suggests that the investment is not financially viable, and investors should look for alternative opportunities.

NPV analysis can also be used to compare different investment opportunities and determine which one is the most financially attractive. By calculating the NPV of each investment opportunity, investors can evaluate the expected returns and risks associated with each option and make an informed investment decision.

In conclusion, NPV analysis is a valuable investment analysis tool that can help investors and businesses evaluate potential investment opportunities and make informed investment decisions. It takes into account the time value of money, cash flows, and the cost of capital, and is widely considered to be the most accurate and comprehensive tool for investment analysis.

Internal rate of return (IRR) and its significance

Introduction In investment analysis, the internal rate of return (IRR) is a commonly used financial metric that measures the profitability of an investment. It represents the interest rate at which the net present value (NPV) of an investment is zero. In other words, the IRR is the discount rate at which the present value of the future cash flows from an investment equals its initial cost. This sub-topic will explore the concept of IRR in detail and its significance in investment analysis.

Calculation of IRR The calculation of IRR involves finding the discount rate that makes the NPV of an investment equal to zero. The formula for IRR can be represented as follows:

$$NPV = 0 = CF_0 + CF_1/(1+IRR) + CF_2/(1+IRR)^2 + ... + CF_n/(1+IRR)^n$$

Where: CF_0 = initial cash outflow (cost of investment) CF_1 to CF_n = cash inflows in subsequent periods n = number of periods

The IRR can be calculated using trial and error, or by using software or financial calculators.

Significance of IRR The IRR is a useful tool for evaluating investment opportunities because it provides a measure of the expected rate of return of an investment. The higher the IRR, the more profitable the investment. The IRR can also be compared with the cost of capital or the required rate of return to determine whether an investment is worth pursuing.

IRR is used in capital budgeting to evaluate potential investments. Companies use the IRR to compare the expected return of different projects and choose the one that offers the highest rate of return. The IRR can also be used to assess the financial viability of a project, as it provides an estimate of the rate of return required to cover the cost of the investment.

Advantages and Limitations of IRR One advantage of IRR is that it considers the time value of money and provides a single rate of return that summarizes the entire investment. It also accounts for the size and timing of cash flows, making it a more accurate measure of profitability than other metrics like the payback period.

However, there are some limitations to using IRR as a measure of investment profitability. One limitation is that it assumes that all cash flows are reinvested at the IRR, which may not always be realistic. IRR also assumes that cash flows are evenly spaced over time, which may not be the case in some investments. Additionally, IRR may not always provide a clear answer in situations where there are multiple cash flow changes or complex investment structures.

Conclusion The internal rate of return is a useful tool for evaluating the profitability of investments. It considers the time value of money and provides a single rate of return that summarizes the entire investment. However, it is important to be aware of the limitations of IRR and to use it in conjunction with other financial metrics to make informed investment decisions.

Payback period and its significance

Introduction One of the key considerations in evaluating an investment opportunity is determining the payback period, which is the length of time it takes for an investment to generate enough cash flows to recoup the initial investment. The payback period is a relatively simple and straightforward metric that can help investors make informed decisions about whether an investment is worthwhile. In this section, we will discuss the significance of the payback period, how it is calculated, and its advantages and disadvantages as an investment analysis tool.

Significance of Payback Period The payback period is a useful metric for several reasons. Firstly, it provides a clear and easily understandable benchmark for evaluating investment opportunities. By calculating the payback period, investors can determine the length of time it will take for an investment to become profitable, which can help them decide whether it is worth pursuing. Secondly, the payback period is a relatively simple and easy-to-calculate metric, which means that investors can use it to quickly evaluate multiple investment opportunities and make informed decisions.

Calculation of Payback Period The payback period is calculated by dividing the initial investment by the average annual cash inflows generated by the investment. For example, if an investment requires an initial investment of $100,000 and generates average annual cash inflows of $25,000, the payback period would be 4 years ($100,000 divided by $25,000).

Advantages of Payback Period One of the key advantages of the payback period is that it is a simple and easy-to-calculate metric that does not require complex financial modeling or analysis. This makes it an accessible tool for investors with limited financial expertise or resources. Additionally, the payback period provides a clear and easily understandable benchmark for evaluating investment opportunities, which can help investors make informed decisions about which investments to pursue.

Disadvantages of Payback Period One of the main disadvantages of the payback period is that it does not take into account the time value of money. This means that it does not account for the fact that a dollar received today is worth more than a dollar received in the future due to inflation and the opportunity cost of not being able to invest that dollar elsewhere. As a result, the payback period may not accurately reflect the true profitability of an investment. Additionally, the payback period does not consider cash flows beyond the payback period, which may be important in evaluating the long-term viability of an investment.

Conclusion The payback period is a useful metric for evaluating investment opportunities, as it provides a clear and easily understandable benchmark for determining the length of time it will take for an investment to become profitable. While the payback period is a relatively simple and accessible tool for investors, it has some limitations and should be used in conjunction with other investment analysis tools to make informed decisions. Overall, the payback period can be a useful tool for investors, but it is important to consider its advantages and disadvantages in the context of each specific investment opportunity.

Capital budgeting process and its components

Introduction Capital budgeting is a critical process for any organization that involves making investment decisions regarding long-term assets. The process involves evaluating various projects and determining which ones to invest in and which ones to reject. Capital budgeting decisions are essential because they impact an organization's profitability, risk, and growth potential. This chapter will explore the capital budgeting process, its components, and how organizations make investment decisions.

Components of the Capital Budgeting Process

1. Project Identification The first step in the capital budgeting process is to identify potential projects that require investment. Project identification involves reviewing the organization's long-term strategic plan, market trends, and industry forecasts to identify opportunities for growth and expansion. Project identification should be a continuous process to ensure that the organization remains competitive and can take advantage of new opportunities as they arise.

2. Project Evaluation The next step in the capital budgeting process is to evaluate potential projects. Project evaluation involves analyzing the feasibility, risk, and potential return of each project. Various techniques can be used to evaluate projects, including net present value (NPV), internal rate of return (IRR), and payback period.

3. Project Selection Once potential projects have been evaluated, the organization needs to select the projects to invest in. Project selection involves comparing the potential returns of each project against its risk and other factors such as availability of resources, strategic fit, and compatibility with the organization's goals.

4. Project Implementation After selecting the projects to invest in, the organization needs to implement them. Project

implementation involves planning and executing the project to achieve the desired outcomes. This may involve acquiring assets, hiring personnel, and obtaining financing.

5. Project Monitoring and Control Finally, the organization needs to monitor and control the project to ensure that it is progressing as planned. This involves tracking the project's progress, identifying any issues or risks, and taking corrective action if necessary.

Techniques Used in Capital Budgeting

1. Net Present Value (NPV) NPV is a widely used capital budgeting technique that calculates the present value of future cash flows associated with a project. It involves discounting the future cash flows using a predetermined discount rate to account for the time value of money. If the NPV is positive, the project is considered financially viable, and it is recommended to invest in the project. If the NPV is negative, the project is rejected.

2. Internal Rate of Return (IRR) IRR is another widely used capital budgeting technique that calculates the discount rate at which the present value of future cash flows is equal to the initial investment. If the IRR is greater than the organization's cost of capital, the project is considered financially viable, and it is recommended to invest in the project. If the IRR is less than the organization's cost of capital, the project is rejected.

3. Payback Period Payback period is a simple capital budgeting technique that calculates the time it takes for the initial investment to be recovered through the project's cash flows. The payback period is a useful tool for assessing the liquidity of an investment, but it does not account for the time value of money.

Conclusion The capital budgeting process is an essential tool for organizations to make investment decisions regarding long-term assets. The process involves identifying potential projects, evaluating their feasibility, selecting the most promising projects, implementing them, and monitoring their progress. The techniques used in capital budgeting, such as NPV, IRR, and payback period, are critical in evaluating potential projects and making investment decisions. Organizations need to understand the capital budgeting process and use the appropriate techniques to ensure that their investment decisions align with their strategic goals and objectives.

The impact of cryptocurrency on investment analysis

Cryptocurrency is a relatively new asset class that has gained significant attention from investors over the past decade. As a decentralized digital currency, it operates outside the traditional financial system and offers a number of unique features that can impact investment analysis. In this article, we will explore the impact of cryptocurrency on investment analysis and how it affects traditional investment models.

1. Volatility and Risk: One of the most significant ways that cryptocurrency impacts investment analysis is through its volatility and risk profile. Cryptocurrencies such as Bitcoin can experience extreme price fluctuations in a matter of hours or days. While this volatility can present opportunities for high returns, it also exposes investors to significant risk. Traditional investment analysis models such as net present value (NPV) and internal rate of return (IRR) rely on stable, predictable cash flows, which may not be the case for cryptocurrencies.

2. Lack of Fundamental Analysis: Another challenge of incorporating cryptocurrency into investment analysis is the lack of fundamental analysis tools. Unlike traditional companies, cryptocurrencies do not have earnings, revenue, or other traditional financial metrics to analyze. This makes it difficult to perform fundamental analysis on cryptocurrencies and may require a different approach to valuation.

3. Liquidity: Liquidity is another factor that can impact investment analysis, and it plays a significant role in the cryptocurrency market. Cryptocurrencies are traded on exchanges, and the liquidity of these markets can vary widely. This can impact the accuracy of market valuations and introduce additional risk into the investment analysis process.

4. Regulatory Environment: The regulatory environment for cryptocurrency is still evolving, and this can introduce additional risk into investment analysis. Government

regulations can impact the use, adoption, and value of cryptocurrencies, which can impact investment returns. The lack of clear regulations and guidelines can make it difficult to assess the legal and regulatory risks associated with investing in cryptocurrencies.

5. Technology: Finally, the technology behind cryptocurrencies is constantly evolving, and this can impact investment analysis. New blockchain technologies and cryptocurrencies are being developed, which can introduce new investment opportunities and risks. Understanding the technology behind cryptocurrencies is essential to accurately assess the risks and returns associated with investing in these assets.

Overall, the impact of cryptocurrency on investment analysis is significant. While traditional investment analysis models may still be applicable, they may require modification to account for the unique characteristics of cryptocurrencies. Investors need to carefully consider the risks and opportunities associated with investing in cryptocurrencies, including the impact on traditional investment analysis models. As the cryptocurrency market continues to evolve, it is likely that investment analysis models will need to adapt to these changes.

Chapter 6: Financial Modeling
Spreadsheet modeling and its components

Introduction: Spreadsheet modeling is a technique used by finance professionals to analyze and forecast financial information using spreadsheets. It involves creating a model that links financial statements together and can be used to make decisions based on projections. Spreadsheet modeling is an essential skill for financial analysts and is used in many different areas of finance, including corporate finance, investment banking, and portfolio management.

Components of Spreadsheet Modeling: Spreadsheet modeling involves several components that are used to create a comprehensive financial model. These components include:

1. Inputs: Inputs are the data points that are used in the model. These can include financial statements, historical data, projections, and assumptions. Inputs are critical to the accuracy of the model, and it is essential to ensure that they are correct and up-to-date.

2. Formulas: Formulas are used to calculate the outputs of the model. These can include simple arithmetic calculations, such as addition and subtraction, or more complex calculations, such as discounted cash flow analysis. Formulas must be carefully constructed to ensure accuracy and avoid errors in the model.

3. Outputs: Outputs are the results of the model. These can include financial statements, ratios, or other metrics that are used to make decisions. Outputs must be clearly presented and easy to understand to ensure that they are useful to decision-makers.

4. Sensitivity Analysis: Sensitivity analysis is a technique used to test the robustness of the model. It involves varying the inputs to see how they impact the outputs. Sensitivity analysis can help to identify the most critical assumptions in the model

and ensure that the model is robust enough to withstand changes in market conditions.

5. Scenario Analysis: Scenario analysis is a technique used to test the model's performance under different scenarios. It involves creating different scenarios based on changes in assumptions or market conditions. Scenario analysis can help decision-makers to identify potential risks and opportunities and make better-informed decisions.

Benefits of Spreadsheet Modeling: Spreadsheet modeling offers several benefits to finance professionals, including:

1. Improved Decision Making: Spreadsheet modeling enables decision-makers to make better-informed decisions by providing accurate and reliable financial information. The model can be used to test different scenarios and assess the impact of various factors on the company's financial performance.

2. Increased Efficiency: Spreadsheet modeling can help finance professionals to work more efficiently by automating calculations and reducing the time required to analyze financial data. This can free up time for more strategic tasks, such as developing investment strategies or analyzing market trends.

3. Better Communication: Spreadsheet modeling can improve communication between finance professionals and other stakeholders, such as management or investors. The model can be used to present financial information in a clear and concise manner, making it easier for stakeholders to understand and make decisions.

4. More Accurate Projections: Spreadsheet modeling can provide more accurate projections of a company's financial performance by incorporating historical data, market trends, and other factors. This can help decision-makers to identify

potential risks and opportunities and make more informed decisions.

Conclusion: Spreadsheet modeling is an essential skill for finance professionals and is used in many different areas of finance. It involves several components, including inputs, formulas, outputs, sensitivity analysis, and scenario analysis. Spreadsheet modeling offers several benefits, including improved decision-making, increased efficiency, better communication, and more accurate projections. Finance professionals must develop and maintain their spreadsheet modeling skills to ensure that they can make informed decisions and succeed in their careers.

Monte Carlo simulation and its components

Monte Carlo simulation is a statistical method used to model and simulate complex systems and processes that involve a significant degree of uncertainty. This simulation technique uses random sampling of input variables to predict the possible outcomes of a decision or event. In finance, Monte Carlo simulation is often used to model the behavior of financial instruments, such as stocks and bonds, and to estimate the potential outcomes of investment decisions.

Monte Carlo simulation involves four main components: input variables, a model or formula, a random number generator, and an output analysis. The input variables are the factors that influence the model's outcome and are often based on historical data or expert estimates. These input variables are assigned probability distributions that represent the degree of uncertainty associated with each variable.

The model or formula is a mathematical representation of the relationship between the input variables and the output variable. The formula can be simple or complex, depending on the nature of the problem being modeled. The random number generator is used to generate random values for the input variables based on their probability distributions.

The output analysis involves running the simulation many times to generate a range of possible outcomes. Each simulation run involves generating a new set of random values for the input variables, using the formula to calculate the output variable, and storing the results. After running the simulation many times, the results are analyzed to determine the range of possible outcomes and their associated probabilities.

Monte Carlo simulation has many applications in finance. For example, it can be used to estimate the expected return and risk of a portfolio of investments or to model the potential impact of market fluctuations on a financial instrument. It can also be used to estimate the probability of meeting a specific financial goal, such as saving enough for retirement.

One advantage of Monte Carlo simulation is its ability to model complex systems and processes with a high degree of accuracy. It also provides a range of possible outcomes, rather than a single point estimate, which can help decision-makers make more informed choices. Additionally, Monte Carlo simulation can help identify potential risks and uncertainties associated with a particular decision or investment.

However, Monte Carlo simulation has some limitations. One of the main challenges is the requirement for accurate input data and probability distributions. If the input data is inaccurate or the probability distributions are not well-defined, the results of the simulation may not be reliable. Additionally, Monte Carlo simulation can be computationally intensive and time-consuming, particularly when modeling complex systems.

In conclusion, Monte Carlo simulation is a powerful tool for modeling and analyzing financial systems and processes. It provides decision-makers with a range of possible outcomes and can help identify potential risks and uncertainties associated with a particular decision or investment. While there are some challenges associated with Monte Carlo simulation, it remains an important technique for financial modeling and analysis.

Sensitivity analysis and its components

Introduction Sensitivity analysis is a crucial tool in financial modeling that helps in measuring the impact of changes in input variables on the output variables of a financial model. It involves testing different scenarios and analyzing the effect of each scenario on the model's output. This analysis enables financial analysts and decision-makers to understand the potential risks and uncertainties involved in financial decisions and helps them make informed decisions. This article will discuss sensitivity analysis in financial modeling, its components, and how it is used in decision-making.

Components of Sensitivity Analysis There are three main components of sensitivity analysis in financial modeling: variable selection, model construction, and scenario analysis.

Variable Selection The first step in sensitivity analysis is identifying the variables that impact the output of the model. These variables are referred to as the input variables. Examples of input variables in a financial model include interest rates, inflation rates, sales volume, and production costs. Once the input variables are identified, their ranges are established, and assumptions are made about their behavior over time.

Model Construction The second component of sensitivity analysis involves constructing the financial model. The model should be designed to capture the relationships between the input variables and the output variable. The model should be flexible and able to handle changes in the input variables. Typically, sensitivity analysis involves using spreadsheets to construct the financial model.

Scenario Analysis Scenario analysis is the final component of sensitivity analysis. It involves testing different scenarios and analyzing the impact of each scenario on the output variable of the financial model. Scenarios are created by varying one or more input variables and observing the resulting change in the output variable. The results of the scenario analysis are presented in a sensitivity table, also known as a tornado chart.

Uses of Sensitivity Analysis Sensitivity analysis is used in financial modeling for various purposes, including risk assessment, decision-making, and forecasting.

Risk Assessment Sensitivity analysis helps in assessing the risk associated with financial decisions. By testing different scenarios, analysts can identify the potential risks and uncertainties involved in a particular decision. This helps in evaluating the potential downside of a decision and designing appropriate risk management strategies.

Decision-Making Sensitivity analysis is used in decision-making to evaluate the impact of different scenarios on the output variable of a financial model. This helps in selecting the most appropriate decision based on the potential outcomes of each scenario.

Forecasting Sensitivity analysis is also used in forecasting to evaluate the impact of changes in input variables on the output variable of a financial model. By testing different scenarios, analysts can evaluate the potential impact of changes in the business environment on the organization's financial performance.

Conclusion Sensitivity analysis is a powerful tool in financial modeling that helps in assessing the potential risks and uncertainties involved in financial decisions. It involves identifying the input variables, constructing the financial model, and testing different scenarios to evaluate the impact of each scenario on the output variable. Sensitivity analysis is used in risk assessment, decision-making, and forecasting and enables financial analysts and decision-makers to make informed decisions.

Forecasting and its components

Introduction: Forecasting is the process of predicting future events or trends based on historical data, statistical analysis, and other relevant information. Financial forecasting is essential for businesses to plan their future operations, allocate resources, and make informed decisions. This chapter will discuss the components of forecasting and the techniques used for forecasting in financial modeling.

Components of Forecasting:

1. Data Analysis: The first step in forecasting is to analyze historical data. Historical data provides a baseline for predicting future trends. In financial forecasting, this includes analyzing financial statements, sales data, customer behavior, and other relevant data.

2. Assumptions: After analyzing the historical data, assumptions are made about future events or trends. Assumptions are based on factors that may influence future trends, such as economic indicators, industry trends, and company-specific factors.

3. Time Horizon: Forecasting requires a time horizon, which is the period over which predictions are made. The time horizon can be short-term, medium-term, or long-term, depending on the purpose of the forecast. Short-term forecasts may cover the next few weeks or months, while long-term forecasts may cover several years.

4. Forecasting Techniques: There are several techniques used in financial forecasting, including time series analysis, regression analysis, and scenario analysis.

Techniques Used in Forecasting:

1. Time Series Analysis: Time series analysis is a statistical technique used to analyze trends and patterns in historical data. This technique is useful for predicting future trends, such as sales growth or revenue growth. Time series

analysis is based on the assumption that past trends will continue into the future.

2. Regression Analysis: Regression analysis is a statistical technique used to analyze the relationship between two or more variables. This technique is useful for predicting future outcomes based on the relationship between variables. For example, regression analysis can be used to predict sales based on marketing spend.

3. Scenario Analysis: Scenario analysis is a technique used to analyze the impact of different scenarios on financial outcomes. This technique involves creating multiple scenarios based on different assumptions, such as economic conditions, customer behavior, and industry trends.

Conclusion: Forecasting is an essential component of financial modeling. It involves analyzing historical data, making assumptions, and using statistical techniques to predict future trends. Financial forecasts are used by businesses to plan their future operations, allocate resources, and make informed decisions. The components of forecasting and the techniques used in financial forecasting are essential for businesses to succeed in today's competitive environment.

The role of blockchain and cryptocurrency in financial modeling

The advent of blockchain technology and cryptocurrency has disrupted the financial modeling space, offering new opportunities for financial analysts and investors. This section explores the role of blockchain and cryptocurrency in financial modeling.

Blockchain technology is a decentralized ledger system that records transactions in a secure and transparent manner. The technology provides a tamper-proof record of all transactions, eliminating the need for a central authority to verify and approve transactions. As a result, blockchain technology has the potential to significantly reduce transaction costs and increase efficiency in financial modeling.

Cryptocurrency is a digital currency that operates on a blockchain network. Cryptocurrency transactions are recorded on a public ledger, providing transparency and immutability. Cryptocurrency has emerged as an alternative to traditional currencies and financial instruments, offering benefits such as low transaction fees, quick settlement times, and increased privacy.

The role of blockchain and cryptocurrency in financial modeling is primarily focused on three areas: portfolio management, risk management, and valuation.

Portfolio management involves the selection and management of a portfolio of assets to achieve investment objectives. Blockchain technology and cryptocurrency offer new opportunities for portfolio management by providing access to new asset classes and markets. For example, investors can use cryptocurrency exchanges to buy and sell cryptocurrencies, providing exposure to a new asset class. Blockchain technology also enables the creation of decentralized finance (DeFi) platforms, which allow investors to earn yield on their cryptocurrency holdings through lending and borrowing activities.

Risk management involves the identification and mitigation of risks associated with investments. Blockchain technology and cryptocurrency offer new tools for risk management by providing transparent and tamper-proof records of transactions. This allows for better tracking and monitoring of investment activities, reducing the risk of fraud and errors. Cryptocurrency also offers new hedging opportunities, such as the use of stablecoins to hedge against cryptocurrency volatility.

Valuation involves the process of determining the intrinsic value of an asset or investment. Blockchain technology and cryptocurrency offer new opportunities for valuation by providing transparent and tamper-proof records of transactions, enabling better tracking and analysis of market data. Cryptocurrency also offers new valuation models, such as the use of network value-to-transactions (NVT) ratios to measure the value of a cryptocurrency network.

One of the main advantages of using blockchain technology and cryptocurrency in financial modeling is increased transparency. Blockchain technology provides a tamper-proof record of all transactions, which can be accessed by anyone with an internet connection. This enables investors and financial analysts to access real-time market data and make informed investment decisions. Additionally, cryptocurrency transactions are settled in real-time, providing quicker access to funds and reducing settlement times.

Another advantage of using blockchain technology and cryptocurrency in financial modeling is increased efficiency. Blockchain technology eliminates the need for a central authority to verify and approve transactions, reducing transaction costs and increasing efficiency. Additionally, cryptocurrency transactions are settled in real-time, providing quicker access to funds and reducing settlement times.

However, there are also challenges associated with using blockchain technology and cryptocurrency in financial modeling. One challenge is the lack of regulation in the cryptocurrency market, which can lead to market volatility and increased risk. Additionally, the use of blockchain technology and cryptocurrency requires a level of technical knowledge and expertise that may not be accessible to all investors and financial analysts.

In conclusion, the role of blockchain technology and cryptocurrency in financial modeling is evolving rapidly. While there are challenges associated with the use of these technologies, they also offer new opportunities for portfolio management, risk management, and valuation. As the adoption of blockchain technology and cryptocurrency continues to grow, financial analysts and investors will need to stay up-to-date on the latest developments and tools to stay competitive in the ever-changing financial modeling space.

Conclusion
Summary of the main points

As we conclude this study on the key concepts of finance and economics, it is important to summarize the main points covered throughout the book. The field of finance and economics is a vast and dynamic one that is constantly evolving to meet the changing demands of the global economy. The aim of this book has been to provide a comprehensive overview of the fundamental concepts and principles that underlie the field, highlighting their significance in contemporary financial analysis and decision-making.

One of the key takeaways from this study is the importance of financial statements as a tool for assessing the financial health of an organization. The balance sheet, income statement, and cash flow statement are critical components of financial analysis, providing valuable insights into an organization's profitability, liquidity, and overall financial stability. The study of financial ratios, such as liquidity ratios, profitability ratios, and solvency ratios, is also an essential part of financial analysis, helping to evaluate an organization's financial performance and identify areas for improvement.

Investment analysis is another important aspect of finance covered in this book. The net present value (NPV), internal rate of return (IRR), and payback period are commonly used techniques for evaluating the potential return on an investment. The capital budgeting process is a critical step in investment analysis, helping to ensure that investment decisions are based on sound financial principles and aligned with an organization's overall strategic goals.

Financial modeling is an essential tool for financial analysis and decision-making, providing a framework for forecasting future financial performance and identifying potential risks and opportunities. Spreadsheet modeling, Monte

Carlo simulation, and sensitivity analysis are all important techniques used in financial modeling. Forecasting is a critical part of financial modeling, helping to predict future trends and outcomes based on past performance and external factors.

Finally, the impact of blockchain and cryptocurrency on finance and economics cannot be overlooked. Blockchain technology has the potential to revolutionize financial transactions and reduce costs, while cryptocurrency is disrupting traditional payment systems and creating new investment opportunities. It is essential for financial analysts and decision-makers to understand these emerging technologies and their implications for the future of finance.

In conclusion, this book has provided a comprehensive overview of the key concepts and principles that underlie the field of finance and economics. From financial statements and investment analysis to financial modeling and the impact of blockchain and cryptocurrency, the topics covered in this book are essential for anyone seeking to gain a deeper understanding of finance and economics. As the field continues to evolve and new technologies emerge, it is essential to stay up-to-date with the latest developments and trends in order to make informed decisions and drive business success.

Implications for the readers

After going through the various topics discussed in this book, it is clear that understanding the principles of microeconomics and financial analysis is crucial for making informed decisions in the business world. In this section, we will explore the implications of this knowledge for the readers of this book.

1. Improved Decision-Making:

One of the main implications of the knowledge gained from this book is the ability to make better decisions. By understanding the various microeconomic principles, readers will be able to make informed decisions about the pricing of goods and services, production levels, and resource allocation. This knowledge is also important for investors, who can use financial analysis to determine the value of potential investments and make informed decisions about where to allocate their funds.

2. Improved Financial Management:

Financial analysis is a critical component of financial management, and readers who understand the various financial statements, ratios, and methods of analysis discussed in this book will be better equipped to manage the financial health of their business or investments. By being able to interpret financial statements and ratios, readers can identify areas of weakness in their financial performance and take corrective action to improve their financial position.

3. Understanding Blockchain and Cryptocurrency:

Blockchain and cryptocurrency are disruptive technologies that have the potential to transform the way we conduct business and manage financial transactions. Readers who understand the basics of blockchain technology and cryptocurrency will be better equipped to take advantage of these innovations in their businesses or investments. They can explore the potential benefits of using blockchain technology to improve supply chain management, reduce transaction costs, and increase transparency and security in financial transactions.

4. Greater Awareness of Economic Issues:

Finally, the knowledge gained from this book will also increase readers' awareness of economic issues that affect the business world. For example, understanding the principles of supply and demand, elasticity, and market structures will allow readers to better understand the impact of economic policies on their business or investments. This knowledge can also help readers identify opportunities for growth and expansion in the market.

In conclusion, the knowledge gained from this book has numerous implications for readers. By understanding the principles of microeconomics and financial analysis, readers can make better decisions, improve financial management, understand disruptive technologies such as blockchain and cryptocurrency, and have a greater awareness of economic issues affecting their business or investments. Overall, this knowledge will enable readers to achieve greater success in their business and investment endeavors.

Insights into the future of finance and economics, including blockchain, digital assets, and cryptocurrency

The world of finance and economics is rapidly evolving, and the rise of blockchain technology, digital assets, and cryptocurrency is changing the game. In this section, we will explore some of the key insights into the future of finance and economics, including the potential impact of blockchain technology and the rise of digital assets and cryptocurrencies.

Blockchain technology is transforming the way financial transactions are conducted. The blockchain is a decentralized digital ledger that allows for secure and transparent transactions without the need for intermediaries. This technology has the potential to revolutionize the financial industry by increasing transparency, reducing fraud and corruption, and improving the speed and efficiency of transactions. With the rise of blockchain, we are seeing the emergence of new financial instruments and services that were previously impossible or impractical.

Digital assets, such as cryptocurrencies, are becoming increasingly popular as a store of value and a means of exchange. Cryptocurrencies are digital or virtual tokens that use cryptography to secure and verify transactions and to control the creation of new units. The rise of cryptocurrencies has created new investment opportunities, as well as new challenges for regulators and policymakers. The decentralized nature of cryptocurrencies and the lack of a central authority make them difficult to regulate and monitor, and there is still much uncertainty surrounding their long-term viability and stability.

Despite the challenges and uncertainties surrounding blockchain, digital assets, and cryptocurrencies, the potential benefits are significant. The emergence of these new technologies is forcing traditional financial institutions to adapt and innovate, which could ultimately lead to a more efficient and inclusive financial system. Furthermore, these technologies have the potential to empower individuals and communities by providing greater access to financial services and by reducing the power of centralized authorities.

As we look to the future of finance and economics, it is clear that blockchain, digital assets, and cryptocurrencies will play an increasingly important role. While there are still many unanswered questions and challenges to be addressed, the potential benefits of these new technologies are undeniable. It is up to policymakers, regulators, and market participants to work together to ensure that these technologies are developed and implemented in a way that maximizes their potential while minimizing their risks.

Call to action

In conclusion, the world of finance and economics is constantly evolving and changing with the advent of new technologies such as blockchain, digital assets, and cryptocurrency. As a reader of this book, it is important to stay up-to-date with these changes and understand their implications for the future of finance.

To take action, consider the following steps:

1. Stay informed: Stay updated on the latest news and trends in finance and economics. Follow reputable sources, such as industry leaders, financial publications, and academic journals, to gain insights into emerging technologies and trends.

2. Learn more about blockchain, digital assets, and cryptocurrency: These technologies have the potential to revolutionize the financial industry. By learning more about them, you can stay ahead of the curve and identify opportunities to invest and innovate.

3. Develop financial modeling skills: Financial modeling is a critical skill for anyone in the finance industry. By developing your modeling skills, you can better analyze and forecast financial data, leading to more informed decisions and better outcomes.

4. Collaborate and network: Connect with other professionals in the industry to share knowledge and insights. Attend industry events, join professional organizations, and participate in online forums to build your network and stay informed.

5. Embrace innovation: The future of finance and economics is driven by innovation. Be open to new ideas and technologies, and look for opportunities to apply them in your work.

By taking these steps, you can become a more informed and effective participant in the world of finance and economics, and help shape its future.

THE END

Key Formulas
Finance and Economics Formulas and Definitions organized according to the topics

Chapter 1: Macroeconomic Parameters

Gross Domestic Product (GDP): the total value of goods and services produced within a country's borders in a specific period. GDP formula: GDP = C + I + G + (X-M), where C is consumption, I is investment, G is government spending, X is exports, and M is imports.

Inflation: the rate at which the general level of prices for goods and services is rising, resulting in a decrease in purchasing power. Inflation formula: ((Current CPI - Base Year CPI) / Base Year CPI) x 100, where CPI is the consumer price index.

Deflation: the opposite of inflation, resulting in an increase in purchasing power.

Unemployment rate: the percentage of the labor force that is unemployed but actively seeking employment. Unemployment rate formula: (Number of unemployed / Labor force) x 100.

Balance of payments: the record of all economic transactions between a country and the rest of the world. Balance of payments formula: Current Account + Capital Account + Financial Account = 0.

Chapter 2: Financial Parameters

Interest rates: the rate at which interest is paid by a borrower for the use of money that they borrow from a lender.

Time value of money: the principle that a dollar today is worth more than a dollar in the future.

Present value: the value of a future amount of money or stream of cash flows, discounted to the present. Present value formula: $PV = FV / (1 + r)^n$, where PV is present value, FV is future value, r is the discount rate, and n is the number of periods.

Future value: the value of an asset or cash at a specified date in the future, based on an assumed rate of growth. Future value formula: $FV = PV \times (1 + r)^n$, where FV is future value, PV is present value, r is the interest rate, and n is the number of periods.

Capital asset pricing model (CAPM): a model that describes the relationship between expected returns and risk for assets. CAPM formula: $E(Ri) = Rf + \beta i(E(Rm) - Rf)$, where E(Ri) is the expected return of the asset, Rf is the risk-free rate, βi is the asset's beta, E(Rm) is the expected return of the market, and (E(Rm) - Rf) is the market risk premium.

Chapter 3: Microeconomic Parameters

Marginal utility: the additional satisfaction or benefit a consumer derives from consuming one additional unit of a good or service.

Marginal cost: the additional cost incurred when producing one additional unit of a good or service.

Production function: a function that describes the relationship between inputs and outputs in the production of goods and services.

Market structures: the different types of markets in which firms operate, including perfect competition, monopolistic competition, oligopoly, and monopoly.

Price elasticity of demand: the degree of responsiveness of quantity demanded to a change in price. Price elasticity of demand formula: (% change in quantity demanded / % change in price).

Chapter 4: Financial Statements

Balance sheet: a financial statement that reports a company's assets, liabilities, and equity at a specific point in time.

Income statement: a financial statement that reports a company's revenue, expenses, and net income over a specific period.

Cash flow statement: a financial statement that reports a company's cash inflows and outflows over a specific period.

Financial ratios: quantitative metrics used to assess a company's financial performance and health

Balance Sheet:

Assets = Liabilities + Equity

Income Statement:

Revenue - Expenses = Net Income

Cash Flow Statement:

Cash from Operations + Cash from Investing + Cash from Financing = Change in Cash

Financial Ratios:

Current Ratio = Current Assets / Current Liabilities

Quick Ratio = (Current Assets - Inventory) / Current Liabilities

Debt-to-Equity Ratio = Total Debt / Total Equity

Gross Margin = Gross Profit / Revenue

Net Margin = Net Income / Revenue

Return on Assets (ROA) = Net Income / Total Assets

Return on Equity (ROE)

Chapter 5: Investment Analysis

Net Present Value (NPV) = $\sum [CF_t / (1+r)t] - C_o$

where CFt = cash flow in time period t

r = discount rate

Co = initial investment

Internal Rate of Return (IRR) = discount rate at which NPV = 0

Payback Period = time period required to recover the initial investment

Payback Period = Co / CF1, where CF1 is the cash flow in the first year

Capital Budgeting Process = the process of making decisions about long-term investments

The process includes identifying potential investments, estimating their cash flows, and analyzing their financial feasibility.

Cryptocurrency = a digital or virtual currency that uses cryptography for security and operates independently of a central bank.

Chapter 6: Financial Modeling

Spreadsheet Modeling = the process of building models in spreadsheets to analyze financial data and make predictions.

Monte Carlo Simulation = a statistical method used to model the probability of different outcomes in a process that cannot easily be predicted due to the intervention of random variables.

Sensitivity Analysis = a technique used to determine how different values of an independent variable affect a particular dependent variable under a given set of assumptions.

Forecasting = the process of making predictions about future events based on historical data and trends.

Blockchain = a decentralized, distributed ledger technology that is used to record transactions across many computers so that the record cannot be altered retroactively without the alteration of all subsequent blocks and the consensus of the network.

Cryptocurrency = a digital or virtual currency that uses cryptography for security and operates independently of a central bank.

Digital Assets = assets that exist in digital form and are typically traded on online platforms. Examples include cryptocurrencies, digital securities, and non-fungible tokens (NFTs).

Additional Financial and Economic Formulas and Parameters

These below are some additional financial and economic formulas and parameters, along with their definitions:

Compound interest: $A = P(1 + r/n)^{(nt)}$

A = final amount

P = principal amount

r = annual interest rate (as a decimal)

n = number of times interest is compounded per year

t = time in years

Rule of 72: Doubling time = 72 / interest rate

This formula is used to estimate the number of years it will take for an investment to double in value at a given interest rate.

Debt-to-income ratio: Total monthly debt payments / gross monthly income

This parameter is used by lenders to assess a borrower's ability to repay debt. A higher debt-to-income ratio indicates that the borrower may have difficulty repaying the debt.

Net worth: Assets - liabilities

Net worth is a measure of an individual's financial health. It represents the value of their assets (such as property, investments, and savings) minus their liabilities (such as mortgages, loans, and credit card debt).

Price-to-earnings ratio (P/E ratio): Market price per share / earnings per share

The P/E ratio is a valuation metric used to assess a company's stock price relative to its earnings. A high P/E ratio may indicate that a company is overvalued, while a low P/E ratio may indicate that it is undervalued.

Return on investment (ROI): (Gain from investment - Cost of investment) / Cost of investment

ROI is a measure of the profitability of an investment. It calculates the return earned on an investment relative to the cost of that investment.

Budget variance: Actual cost - Budgeted cost

Budget variance is a measure of the difference between the actual cost of a project or activity and the budgeted cost. A positive budget variance indicates that the project or activity came in under budget, while a negative budget variance indicates that it exceeded the budget.

Elasticity of demand: % change in quantity demanded / % change in price

Elasticity of demand measures the responsiveness of demand for a product or service to changes in its price. If the elasticity of demand is greater than 1, demand is considered to be elastic, meaning that a small change in price will result in a large change in quantity demanded. If the elasticity of demand is less than 1, demand is considered to be inelastic, meaning that a change in price will have little effect on quantity demanded.

Marginal revenue: Change in revenue / Change in quantity

Marginal revenue is the additional revenue generated by selling one more unit of a product or service. It is calculated as the change in revenue divided by the change in quantity.

Time horizons: Short-term, medium-term, and long-term

Time horizons are used to describe the length of time over which a particular investment or financial decision is expected to have an impact. Short-term investments or decisions typically have a time horizon of less than one year, while medium-term investments or decisions have a time horizon of one to five years, and long-term investments or decisions have a time horizon of more than five years.

Debt-to-Income Ratio (DTI) = Total Debt Payments / Gross Monthly Income

DTI is a financial parameter that represents the percentage of a person's gross monthly income that goes towards paying off their debts. It is used by lenders to assess a borrower's ability to repay a loan.

Rule of 72 = 72 / Interest Rate

The rule of 72 is a quick and easy way to estimate how long it will take for an investment to double in value, given a fixed annual interest rate.

Sharpe Ratio = (Portfolio Return - Risk-Free Rate) / Portfolio Standard Deviation

The Sharpe ratio is a measure of risk-adjusted performance that evaluates the return of an investment relative to its risk.

Price-to-Earnings (P/E) Ratio = Price per Share / Earnings per Share

The P/E ratio is a financial parameter used to evaluate a company's stock price relative to its earnings. It is calculated by dividing the price per share by the earnings per share.

Net Working Capital = Current Assets - Current Liabilities

Net working capital is a financial parameter that represents the amount of a company's current assets that are available to cover its current liabilities.

Compound Interest Formula – $P(1+r/n)^{(nt)}$

The compound interest formula is used to calculate the future value of an investment that earns compound interest. It takes into account the principal amount, interest rate, compounding frequency, and time period.

Present Value Formula = $FV / (1+r)^t$

The present value formula is used to calculate the current value of a future sum of money, based on a discount rate and a specific time period.

Expected Value = (Probability of Success x Potential Gain) - (Probability of Failure x Potential Loss)

The expected value is a financial parameter that represents the average outcome of a probabilistic event, taking into account the potential gains and losses involved.

Debt Service Coverage Ratio (DSCR) = Net Operating Income / Total Debt Service

The DSCR is a financial parameter used to evaluate the ability of a business to cover its debt obligations. It is calculated by dividing the net operating income by the total debt service.

Economic Order Quantity (EOQ) = sqrt((2DS)/H)

The EOQ is a formula used in inventory management to determine the optimal order quantity that minimizes total inventory costs. It takes into account the demand rate, setup cost, holding cost, and order cost.

Debt-to-Equity Ratio: A financial ratio that compares a company's total debt to its total equity. It is calculated by dividing total debt by total equity.

Return on Investment (ROI): A performance measure used to evaluate the efficiency of an investment. It is calculated by dividing the net profit of an investment by its cost.

Net Asset Value (NAV): The value of a mutual fund or exchange-traded fund (ETF) per share. It is calculated by subtracting the fund's liabilities from its assets and dividing the result by the number of outstanding shares.

Compound Interest: Interest that is earned on both the principal amount and any accumulated interest from previous periods. It is calculated by multiplying the principal amount by the interest rate, then adding the interest earned and continuing the calculation for each period.

Price-Earnings Ratio (P/E Ratio): A valuation ratio used to compare a company's current share price to its earnings per share. It is calculated by dividing the current share price by the earnings per share.

Cost of Goods Sold (COGS): The direct costs associated with producing a product or providing a service. It includes the cost of materials and labor used in production.

Current Ratio: A financial ratio that compares a company's current assets to its current liabilities. It is calculated by dividing current assets by current liabilities.

Gross Margin: The difference between a company's revenue and its cost of goods sold, expressed as a percentage of revenue. It is calculated by subtracting the cost of goods sold from the revenue, then dividing the result by the revenue.

Operating Margin: A financial ratio that measures a company's operating income as a percentage of its revenue. It is calculated by dividing operating income by revenue.

Price-Sales Ratio: A valuation ratio that compares a company's market capitalization to its revenue. It is calculated by dividing the company's market capitalization by its revenue.

Return on Investment (ROI) = (Gain from Investment - Cost of Investment) / Cost of Investment: ROI measures the profitability of an investment.

Compound Annual Growth Rate (CAGR) = [(Ending Value / Beginning Value)^(1 / Number of Years)] - 1: CAGR measures the average annual growth rate of an investment over a period of time.

Debt-to-Equity Ratio = Total Debt / Total Equity: This ratio compares a company's total debt to its total equity and is used to assess its financial leverage.

Dividend Yield = Annual Dividend per Share / Current Stock Price: Dividend yield measures the return on investment of a stock based on the dividend paid.

Price-to-Earnings Ratio (P/E Ratio) = Current Stock Price / Earnings per Share (EPS): P/E ratio is a valuation ratio used to determine the relative value of a company's shares based on its earnings.

Quick Ratio = (Current Assets - Inventory) / Current Liabilities: Quick ratio measures a company's ability to pay off its short-term debts with its most liquid assets.

Debt Coverage Ratio = Net Operating Income / Total Debt Service: This ratio measures a company's ability to cover its debt obligations.

Time to Double = 72 / Annual Interest Rate: Time to double is a rule of thumb used to estimate how long it takes an investment to double in value at a given interest rate.

Weighted Average Cost of Capital (WACC) = (Cost of Equity x % of Equity) + (Cost of Debt x % of Debt x (1 - Tax Rate)) + (Cost of Preferred Stock x % of Preferred Stock): WACC is a calculation of a company's cost of capital, taking into account the relative proportions of each source of financing.

Rule of 72 = 72 / Interest Rate: The rule of 72 is a quick mental calculation to estimate how long it takes for an investment to double in value at a given interest rate.

Beta = Covariance of Stock Returns with Market Returns / Variance of Market Returns: Beta measures a stock's sensitivity to market risk.

Operating Margin = Operating Income / Net Sales: Operating margin measures a company's operating income as a percentage of its net sales.

Price-to-Sales Ratio (P/S Ratio) = Market Capitalization / Total Revenue: P/S ratio is a valuation ratio used to determine the relative value of a company's shares based on its revenue.

Economic Order Quantity (EOQ) = Square Root of [(2 x Annual Demand x Cost per Order) / Holding Cost per Unit]:

EOQ is used to calculate the optimal quantity of goods to order to minimize total inventory costs.

Present Value (PV) = Future Value / (1 + Interest Rate)^Number of Years: PV is used to determine the current value of a future cash flow.

Debt-to-Equity Ratio = Total Debt / Total Equity

A measure of a company's leverage, indicating the proportion of debt and equity used to finance its assets.

Dividend Yield = Annual Dividend per Share / Stock Price per Share

A measure of the annual return on investment of a stock.

Sharpe Ratio = (Portfolio Return - Risk-Free Rate) / Portfolio Standard Deviation

A measure of the risk-adjusted return of an investment.

P/E Ratio (Price-to-Earnings Ratio) = Stock Price per Share / Earnings per Share

A valuation ratio that compares a company's stock price to its earnings per share.

Capital Asset Pricing Model (CAPM) = Risk-Free Rate + Beta x (Market Return - Risk-Free Rate)

A model that estimates the expected return of an investment based on its risk and the market return.

Price Elasticity of Demand = % Change in Quantity Demanded / % Change in Price

A measure of the responsiveness of quantity demanded to changes in price.

Present Value (PV) = Future Value / (1 + Interest Rate)^n

The current value of a future sum of money, discounted at a given interest rate and time period.

Net Working Capital = Current Assets - Current Liabilities

A measure of a company's liquidity, indicating the amount of cash available for day-to-day operations.

Modified Duration = Macaulay Duration / (1 + Yield to Maturity)

A measure of the sensitivity of a bond's price to changes in interest rates.

Black-Scholes Model = S x N(d1) - X x e^(-rT) x N(d2)

A mathematical model used to calculate the theoretical value of options contracts.

Compound Interest Formula: FV = PV x (1 + r/n)^(nt)

FV = future value, PV = present value, r = interest rate, n = number of times interest is compounded per year, t = time in years

Debt-to-Equity Ratio Formula: D/E = Total Debt / Total Equity

D/E = debt-to-equity ratio, Total Debt = total debt of a company, Total Equity = total equity of a company

Dividend Yield Formula: Dividend Yield = Annual Dividend / Stock Price

Dividend Yield = dividend yield, Annual Dividend = total annual dividends paid, Stock Price = current stock price

Return on Investment (ROI) Formula: ROI = (Gain from Investment - Cost of Investment) / Cost of Investment

ROI = return on investment, Gain from Investment = total return from investment, Cost of Investment = total cost of investment

Price-to-Earnings (P/E) Ratio Formula: P/E Ratio = Stock Price / Earnings Per Share (EPS)

P/E Ratio = price-to-earnings ratio, Stock Price = current stock price, EPS = earnings per share

Return on Assets (ROA) Formula: ROA = Net Income / Total Assets

ROA = return on assets, Net Income = total net income of a company, Total Assets = total assets of a company

Present Value of Annuity Formula: PV = C x ((1 - (1 + r)^-n) / r)

PV = present value, C = periodic payment, r = interest rate, n = number of payments

Operating Margin Formula: Operating Margin = Operating Income / Revenue

Operating Margin = operating margin, Operating Income = total operating income, Revenue = total revenue

Quick Ratio Formula: Quick Ratio = (Current Assets - Inventory) / Current Liabilities

Quick Ratio = quick ratio, Current Assets = total current assets, Inventory = total inventory, Current Liabilities = total current liabilities

Economic Order Quantity (EOQ) Formula: EOQ = sqrt((2DS) / H)

EOQ = economic order quantity, D = annual demand, S = ordering cost per order, H = holding cost per unit

Dividend Yield: A financial ratio that indicates how much a company pays out in dividends relative to its stock price. It is calculated by dividing the annual dividend payment by the stock price.

Price-Earnings Ratio (P/E Ratio): A financial ratio that compares a company's stock price to its earnings per share. It is calculated by dividing the stock price by the earnings per share.

Return on Investment (ROI): A performance measure used to evaluate the efficiency of an investment or to compare the efficiency of several different investments. It is calculated by dividing the net profit by the cost of the investment.

Compound Interest: Interest that is calculated on the initial principal and also on the accumulated interest of previous periods. It is calculated by multiplying the principal by the interest rate raised to the number of compounding periods.

Debt-to-Equity Ratio: A financial ratio that compares a company's total debt to its total equity. It is calculated by dividing the total debt by the total equity.

Time Horizon: The length of time over which an investment is held before it is sold. It is an important consideration when determining the appropriate investment strategy.

Risk-Adjusted Return: A measure of the return earned on an investment relative to the risk associated with that investment. It is calculated by dividing the excess return by the standard deviation of returns.

Asset Allocation: The process of dividing an investment portfolio among different asset categories, such as stocks, bonds, and cash. It is based on the investor's goals, risk tolerance, and investment time horizon.

Present Value of Annuity: The current value of a series of equal cash flows received or paid at regular intervals for a specified period of time. It is calculated by discounting each cash flow to its present value and then adding them up.

Future Value of Annuity: The value of a series of equal cash flows received or paid at regular intervals for a specified period of time, at a specified interest rate. It is calculated by compounding each cash flow to its future value and then adding them up.

Beta: A measure of a stock's volatility relative to the overall market. It is calculated by dividing the covariance between the stock and the market by the variance of the market.

Capital Gains: The profit earned on the sale of an investment. It is calculated by subtracting the purchase price from the sale price.

Liquidity: The degree to which an asset or security can be bought or sold in the market without affecting its price. It is an important consideration when selecting investments.

Yield to Maturity: The rate of return anticipated on a bond if it is held until the maturity date. It is calculated by solving for the interest rate in the bond's present value equation.

Stock Split: A corporate action in which a company divides its existing shares into multiple shares. It is typically done to make the stock more affordable for individual investors.

Market Capitalization: The total value of a company's outstanding shares of stock. It is calculated by multiplying the number of shares by the stock price.

Earnings Per Share (EPS): A company's profit divided by the number of outstanding shares of stock. It is an important metric used to evaluate a company's profitability.

Debt Service Coverage Ratio: A financial ratio that measures a company's ability to repay its debt. It is calculated by dividing the company's net operating income by its total debt service.

Price-Book Ratio: A financial ratio that compares a company's stock price to its book value per share. It is calculated by dividing the stock price by the book value per share.

Return on Equity (ROE) = Net Income / Shareholders' Equity. ROE measures the amount of profit a company generates for each dollar of shareholder's equity.

Debt-to-Equity Ratio = Total Debt / Shareholders' Equity. This ratio measures the amount of debt a company has relative to its equity.

Current Ratio = Current Assets / Current Liabilities. This ratio measures a company's ability to pay its short-term liabilities with its short-term assets.

Acid-Test Ratio (or Quick Ratio) = (Current Assets - Inventory) / Current Liabilities. This ratio measures a company's ability to pay its short-term liabilities with its most liquid assets.

Weighted Average Cost of Capital (WACC) = (Cost of Equity x % Equity) + (Cost of Debt x % Debt) + (Cost of Preferred Stock x % Preferred Stock) x (1 - Tax Rate). This is the average cost of all the capital a company has raised to finance its operations.

DuPont Model = Net Profit Margin x Asset Turnover Ratio x Equity Multiplier. This model breaks down a company's return on equity into three components: profitability, efficiency, and financial leverage.

Capital Asset Pricing Model (CAPM) = Risk-Free Rate + Beta x (Market Rate of Return - Risk-Free Rate). This model calculates the expected return on an asset based on its level of risk.

Black-Scholes Model = (Stock Price x N(d1)) - (Present Value of Exercise Price x N(d2)). This model is used to calculate the theoretical price of an option.

Gordon Growth Model = Dividend per Share / (Discount Rate - Dividend Growth Rate). This model is used to estimate the intrinsic value of a stock based on its current dividend and expected future growth rate.

Sharpe Ratio = (Portfolio Return - Risk-Free Rate) / Portfolio Standard Deviation. This ratio measures the excess return of a portfolio compared to its level of risk.

Glossary

Here are some key terms and definitions related to the topics covered in this book:

1. Asset: An item of economic value owned by an individual or organization that can be used to generate future income.

2. Balance sheet: A financial statement that provides a snapshot of a company's financial position by showing its assets, liabilities, and equity at a specific point in time.

3. Blockchain: A digital ledger that records transactions in a decentralized and secure manner using cryptography.

4. Capital budgeting: The process of determining whether a long-term investment is worth pursuing based on its expected returns and costs.

5. Cash flow: The amount of cash that flows in and out of a business over a specific period of time.

6. Cryptocurrency: A digital or virtual currency that uses cryptography for security and operates independently of a central bank.

7. Financial modeling: The process of creating a mathematical representation of a financial situation or system to help make better decisions.

8. Income statement: A financial statement that shows a company's revenue, expenses, and net income over a specific period of time.

9. Internal rate of return (IRR): The discount rate that makes the net present value of an investment equal to zero.

10. Investment analysis: The process of evaluating potential investments to determine their feasibility, risk, and potential returns.

11. Monte Carlo simulation: A method of modeling uncertain variables in which multiple simulations are run using random inputs to generate a range of possible outcomes.

12. Net present value (NPV): The present value of expected future cash flows minus the cost of the investment.

13. Payback period: The length of time it takes for an investment to generate enough cash flow to recover its initial cost.

14. Sensitivity analysis: The process of examining how changes in input variables affect the output of a financial model.

15. Spreadsheet: A computer program used to organize and analyze data using rows and columns.

16. Time horizon: The length of time over which an investment is expected to generate returns.

These are just some of the key terms and definitions related to the topics covered in this book. Understanding these terms is essential for anyone interested in finance, economics, and investment analysis.

Potential References

Introduction:
Gitman, L. J., & Joehnk, M. D. (2014). Introduction to finance. Cengage Learning.
Chapter 1: Macroeconomic Parameters
Mankiw, N. G. (2014). Principles of macroeconomics. Cengage Learning.
Blanchard, O. (2017). Macroeconomics. Pearson Education.
Chapter 2: Financial Parameters
Brealey, R. A., Myers, S. C., & Allen, F. (2017). Principles of corporate finance. McGraw-Hill Education.
Hull, J. C. (2018). Options, futures, and other derivatives. Pearson Education.
Chapter 3: Microeconomic Parameters
Varian, H. R. (2014). Microeconomic analysis. WW Norton & Company.
Pindyck, R. S., & Rubinfeld, D. L. (2017). Microeconomics. Pearson Education.
Chapter 4: Financial Statements
Penman, S. H. (2013). Financial statement analysis and security valuation. McGraw-Hill Education.
Palepu, K. G., Healy, P. M., & Bernard, V. L. (2016). Business analysis and valuation: Using financial statements. Cengage Learning.
Chapter 5: Investment Analysis
Bodie, Z., Kane, A., & Marcus, A. J. (2018). Investments. McGraw-Hill Education.
Brigham, E. F., & Ehrhardt, M. C. (2013). Financial management: Theory and practice. Cengage Learning.
Chapter 6: Financial Modeling
Simon, H. A., & Blume, L. E. (1994). Mathematics for economists. WW Norton & Company.
Benninga, S. (2018). Financial modeling. MIT Press.

Conclusion:
Thaler, R. H. (2015). Misbehaving: The making of behavioral economics. WW Norton & Company.
Tapscott, D., & Tapscott, A. (2016). Blockchain revolution: How the technology behind bitcoin is changing money, business, and the world. Penguin.

www.ingramcontent.com/pod-product-compliance
Lightning Source LLC
LaVergne TN
LVHW050916200726
843508LV00011B/2210

9 782421 998753